Custer's Road to Disaster

The Path to Little Bighorn

Kevin M. Sullivan

TWODOT®

GUILFORD, CONNECTICUT
HELENA, MONTANA

AN IMPRINT OF GLOBE PEQUOT PRESS

A · **TWODOT®** · **BOOK**

Copyright © 2013 by Kevin M. Sullivan

TwoDot is an imprint of Globe Pequot Press and a registered trademark of Morris Book Publishing, LLC.

Map by Melissa Baker © Morris Book Publishing, LLC
Project editor: Meredith Dias
Layout: Melissa Evarts

Library of Congress Cataloging-in-Publication Data

Sullivan, Kevin M., 1955-
  Custer's road to disaster : the path to Little Bighorn / Kevin M. Sullivan.
     p. cm.
  Includes bibliographical references and index.
  ISBN 978-0-7627-8441-7
  1. Custer, George A. (George Armstrong), 1839-1876. 2. Little Bighorn, Battle of the, Mont., 1876. 3. Generals—United States—Biography. 4. United States. Army—Biography. I. Title.
  E467.1.C99S85 2013
  973.8'2092—dc23
  [B]
                               2012036984

Printed in the United States of America

10 9 8 7 6 5 4 3 2 1

For my grandson,
Connor Jackson Ludwig

Battle of the Little Bighorn – June 25, 1876

Custer's Route

Reno-Benteen
Battlefield Hill

Reno's Retreat

Woods

Reno's Attack

Skirmish
Line

River

Bighorn

Little

Hunkpapa

Medicine Tail Coulee
(Possible site of Custer's Wounding)

Custer's Route

Minneconjou

INDIAN ENCAMPMENT

Blackfeet

Sans Arc

Oglala

Brule

Last Stand
Hill

Cheyenne

Reno Creek

0   0.5   1 kilometer
0   0.5   1 mile

Contents

Acknowledgments

Whenever anyone undertakes to write about the important events of those who are long dead, I believe it is very important to remember those who have gone before us, who have diligently documented the facts and circumstances that surrounded those lives. Without these individuals, much of what we call history would forever be lost to us, and the researcher would have virtually nowhere to go. To the many fine people who contributed to recording the events surrounding the life of George Armstrong Custer, from field reporters to established authors, I thank you. To those among the living who aided me in my search, I am indebted to you in ways you cannot imagine, for in some cases we exchanged words without exchanging names.

I would like to thank specifically the folks at the Armor Library at Fort Knox, Kentucky (now located at Fort Benning, Georgia), for their fine help and assistance. A big round of applause to the fine individuals in the research department at the Louisville Free Public Library, especially those who were forced to retrieve a number of old, dust-covered government publications that hadn't been used in years. I am also indebted to Ms. Sharon A. Small, museum specialist at Little Bighorn Battlefield National Monument, who worked very hard to get me the photographs I needed during a period of transition for the museum. Thanks also to Retired Lieutenant General Harold G. Moore, coauthor of the book, *We Were Soldiers Once . . . and Young,* and the late Brian C. Pohanka, for their very kind words regarding my previous work on George Custer. I would also be remiss if I didn't mention my friend and fellow writer, Ron Franscell, and the pivotal part he played in connecting me with Erin Turner of Globe Pequot Press.

And finally, I would like to offer my eternal gratitude to my wife, Linda Sullivan, who has been with me for every literary journey and working trip, always there to encourage me and offer her assistance in any way possible. With her at my side, the research and writing experience for each book has been an absolute joy.

PREFACE

Much has changed in the world since that day in June 1876 when George Armstrong Custer and five companies of his Seventh Cavalry perished under a broiling Montana sun. Many conflicts, great and small, have occurred over the last 137 years, filling the history books with the names of winners and losers from around the globe. Yet for many Americans, the Battle of Little Bighorn has continued to hold a unique place within our national psyche despite this passage of time. One can study bloodier battles, engaging larger armies and lasting far longer than that which occurred between the US military and the Native Americans on that day. Yet this battle is unique for a number of reasons, all of which would continue to produce changes for both cultures long after the smoke of battle had drifted away from the field.

First, the Indians were under no illusions concerning the final outcome in that summer of 1876, yet they were like anyone else who cherishes freedom and has no desire to go gently into that good night. And so, when Custer came looking for battle, they did not disappoint him. While the defeat of Custer must be considered their greatest victory against the whites, it would be bittersweet, for it would signal quite clearly the beginning of the end of their way of life. After Little Bighorn, a new, determined sense of wrath was kindled among those who sought to end what they considered to be a problem long overdue to be solved. It would be a pivotal battle, destined to radically change both cultures.

In one fell swoop the Sioux and Cheyenne warriors shattered the myth of Custer as the unconquerable warrior. The death of George Armstrong Custer ended the life of one of the most flamboyant, brave, careless, and fascinating characters to ever wear a US military uniform. His dramatic rise during the Civil War to the brevet (or temporary) rank of brigadier general at the tender age of twenty-three, and his uncanny ability to stay alive regardless of how recklessly he flung himself at the enemy, gave rise to his image as an almost mythical figure. Even President Lincoln had heard about this dashing young warrior whose name had become a household word. General Sheridan was so pleased with him that after General Grant and General Lee had signed the formal papers of surrender at Appomattox, Sheridan purchased the table upon which the documents had been signed and gave it to Custer as a gift for his wife. Forever after, Custer would be seen as the darling of the nation. More than anything else, he would be remembered by his generation as the boy general who went from victory to victory, whose life was filled with such good fortune that the term "Custer's Luck" was used to refer to an unusually fortuitous event.

Yet if Custer could rise today from his tomb at West Point, he would be horrified to know that his fame, just a little over a century later, would spring from this very quick battle that resulted not only in his death, but in one of the worst military defeats in US history. Not a great legacy, to be sure, but history never promised it would be kind in remembering us, only to remember.

But what really happened at Little Bighorn, and what thoughts were spilling from the mind of Custer on that fateful day? For Custer, the idea that his beloved Seventh Cavalry would ever be defeated by an untrained, undisciplined, and unorganized group of Plains Indians had never entered his mind. Such arrogant heads had been raised in the US military before, only to be lopped off by untrained, undisciplined, and unorganized (but very determined) warriors.

When, on June 25, 1876, the scout Bloody Knife told Custer that there were more Sioux awaiting them than they had bullets, he merely responded, "Well, I guess we'll get through them in one day." This expectation would evaporate before Custer's eyes in little more time than it takes one to consume a meal, according to one Indian participant.

Custer's miscalculation of the unstoppable power of his regiment would not be the only miscalculation of the campaign. Indeed, it would prove to be one of many. His refusal to heed the advice of his scouts as to the size of the village they were attacking (Custer didn't want negotiations, only a decisive battle) would also contribute to their undoing. His belief that the Indians would flee at the first sign of trouble also proved false, but by the time Custer realized his mistake, his fate was irretrievably sealed. Tragically, his decision to split the regiment guaranteed disaster. Once the command was separated, Custer and his five companies were quickly drawn into the vortex from which there would be no escape.

In light of this, I believe it is fair to say that Custer died not so much from Sioux and Cheyenne bullets as from wrong thinking. As was always the case when he led men into battle, Custer was going to do things his way. What is so ironic is that the Indians had had an ally in Custer, and soon many lives would be sacrificed on the altar of his ignorance. That the command would escape complete annihilation, given the perilous position in which Custer had placed them, is all the more surprising.

To understand Custer the Indian fighter, one must understand the Custer who came charging out of the smoke and fire of the Civil War. By gazing into his years as a youth and watching how the young warrior would develop, it is easy to identify certain character traits that would actually help the Little Bighorn disaster unfold.

Finally, it is my intention in this book to focus on Custer's personality and how he chose to conduct warfare. Keys to the well-known personality traits of Custer the man can be found in Custer the boy, how he evolved within the family setting and responded to the central authority figures in his life. The resounding military defeat of George Armstrong Custer along the Little Bighorn River on an extremely hot day in late June 1876, was in fact a culmination of mitigating factors, all of which aligned themselves to create for Custer's enemy the perfect storm of conflict, and one in which the Plains Indians took great pleasure. One of the greatest factors prevailing on that day, and during the weeks prior to the battle, was Custer's inability to grasp the reality of what was waiting for him.

As we shall see, even the overall sense of doom that pervaded much of the command just before beginning their march did not move him or cause him to ponder their fate. And the dire warnings of his trusted scouts as to the dangers and likely destruction they faced once they attacked the Sioux and Cheyenne were also ignored. At this time, Custer the famed and unconquerable warrior became Custer the pied piper, leading his troops to an early grave.

Even so, the failing of one campaign, no matter how blatant, cannot erase the courage Custer displayed or the accomplishments he achieved during the Civil War. Like all of humanity, Custer was a complex individual and sometimes given to extremes. After years of research, I often find myself drifting somewhere between respect and disgust for the man, and perhaps, in light of the evidence, this is the way it ought to be.

—KEVIN M. SULLIVAN
LOUISVILLE, KENTUCKY

CHAPTER 1

Birth of an Icon

George Armstrong Custer made his entrance into the world on December 5, 1839, in the small hamlet of New Rumley, Ohio. That he was a strong baby is without doubt, and given the mortality rate of the day, this would serve him well in a world where long-term survival was often difficult to achieve. Yet, as we shall see, despite this knowledge of the precariousness of life, Custer never seemed concerned about his own mortality. He would learn to face death time and time again as a young warrior. From his humble beginnings in this small Ohio village to his meteoric rise as a military icon during the Civil War, to his catastrophic and shocking demise at the hands of Plains Indians, there is a uniqueness of being that sets him apart. Admired or despised, there is no denying that George Custer began taking on a mythical status while he was alive, and given the strange and unusual way in which he and his command were destroyed, that mythology has both changed and intensified over the years. His very death has been seared into the American consciousness in a way even this boy general would never have imagined.

Indeed, his was a life that almost wasn't. The marriage of young Custer's parents, Emanuel Henry Custer and Maria Ward Kirkpatrick, became a reality only because of the untimely deaths of their first spouses. Having married Matilda Viers on August 7, 1828, Emanuel Custer was a father of three when his wife died just three weeks shy of their seventh anniversary, leaving the young widower with a broken heart and heavy responsibility.[1] Within seven months, however, Emanuel would find another chance at happiness in the person of Maria Ward Kirkpatrick, and on February 23, 1836, the couple was married.[2]

Both newlyweds brought children into the union: Emanuel, three (one would die prior to George's birth) and Maria, two. And of course, it wasn't long before the couple began expanding the family, though their first two children (both sons) would not survive infancy. George Armstrong, however, as if battling the odds, would break this mortal streak, and the successive children to come along would all be robust except one. Indeed, the depressing and untimely deaths of loved ones stopped altogether with the birth of George, and it wouldn't be until the horrific events along the Little Bighorn River, far into the future, that the family would collectively suffer its greatest loss. Nevertheless, in July of 1842, Nevin would be born, and while he was definitely sickly when compared to his siblings (both current and yet to be), he would still manage to outlive them all.[3] Thomas Ward, who in many ways would become his brother's right-hand man and closest confidant, entered the world in 1845, followed by Boston in 1848. Their last child, Margaret (the only daughter born to the couple), took her first breath in 1852.

That they were a large and happy family is without question. Like his father, Emanuel was a blacksmith by trade. He also loved and talked politics constantly, sang in the church, served four terms as justice of the peace, and was a proud member of the Ohio militia. And it would be here, watching his father drill, rifle to shoulder with other men, that young Autie (a nickname George acquired in childhood—his early attempt to pronounce his middle name of "Armstrong") would get his first real taste of military life. Seeing their father marching in step excited Autie and Thomas; they sensed the unmistakable cohesion of a military unit, and it made a deep impression on the young boys.

But Emanuel was not all seriousness; in fact, he was quite the prankster at home. He greatly enjoyed devising practical jokes along with his boys—jokes that were sometimes elaborately played out, even in public. One such episode involved sons Tom and Autie "stealing" Emanuel's wallet while they were traveling together by boat. One evening during the trip, Tom kept insisting that his father go to bed. As the elder Custer detailed it in a letter written years later: "Tommy and I had a stateroom together, and one night in particular, all the folks had gone to bed in the cabin, and Tom was hurrying me to go to bed. I was not sleepy, and did not want to turn in. . . ." Eventually Emanuel did go to bed, and after taking the bottom bunk, Tom slyly observed his father placing his vest and wallet under his pillow. As the elder Custer sat down, Tom grabbed the vest and wallet, and while Emanuel was removing his boots, he threw them over the transom where Autie was waiting. Emanuel, seeing something flying over his head, turned around and pulled back the pillow. One look and the old man knew immediately what had happened. At this same moment, Tom began to feign snoring. Emanuel awakened him to tell him what happened, correctly believing that Autie was responsible for the prank. Rushing out, Emanuel began pounding on the door he believed belonged to Autie. Indeed, the pounding was so loud that doors around him began swinging open, but Autie never appeared. Before Emanuel had a chance to storm off, he heard the scream of a young female, and a pitcher of water was poured over the transom and onto his head. Now soaked, Emanuel returned to his room and gave hell to the only son he could locate, but Tom denied everything.

Early the next morning Autie located his father, and with his best deadpan expression, began asking him about the "fracas" the night before, scolding him for troubling the woman. Autie then told his father he'd knocked on the wrong door, frightened the young woman, and that she had had little choice but to defend herself by attacking him with the water. Emanuel *had* picked the right door, however, and it was Autie who had tossed the pitcher of water and orchestrated the screaming of the female. Later, the old man got his revenge by complaining to a crowd of roughneck boatmen that Autie and Tom were pickpockets, refusing to admit the truth until it appeared some harm might come to his sons.[4]

One might be inclined to believe that such antics were the exception rather than the rule for family life with the Custers, but this was not the case. Anyone in New Rumley who had any dealings with the Custer clan was well aware of this pattern of behavior and knew the type of wild she-nanigans the family was constantly involved in.

This ongoing and good-natured struggle between them—where one trick invited another, perhaps more spectacular one—lasted well into the adulthood of the Custer boys.[5] One such incident took place shortly after the end of the Civil War, when Custer was serving in Texas. Emanuel, having joined Autie and Tom as a foraging agent with the army, must have known he was going to be the butt of jokes. Even so, the brothers were constantly catching him off guard, and Autie put more than a little effort into his quest to fool his father. According to a letter Emanuel penned to his daughter-in-law, Libbie (Autie would marry Libbie Bacon in 1864), Autie was always verbally sparring with his father over politics, taking the latest position of the Republican Party (Emanuel was a Demo-crat), just to get under his skin. Libbie said her husband was often so con-vincing during these discussions that even she had a hard time believing it was all a ruse. So one evening, just as the elder Custer was sitting down to a hot plate of steaming meat and vegetables, Autie burst into the room espousing the latest Republican issue and why he agreed with it, causing Emanuel to jump up from the table and take up the fight to counter the ramblings of his wayward son. Soon he'd forgotten all about his dinner, and while he wasn't looking, Tom crept into the room and ate his food for him.[6]

What is of keen interest here is that by the time these pranks were occurring, both Autie and Tom were battle-hardened soldiers. As such, one might be inclined to question why such overly juvenile activities were still so common within their family. On the one hand, growing up in such an environment no doubt aided young Autie and the other boys in main-taining a youthful outlook on life, which has obvious positive aspects, as they were a very happy and contented lot. Tipping the scale in the other direction, however, is that unmistakable thread of distraction that ran through George Custer—a certain willful disobedience, or even outright rebellion, which kept prompting him to sometimes skirt the rules, both on and off the battlefield. This cavalier attitude toward decision-making, clearly evident in his actions just prior to and during the Little Bighorn campaign, had its genesis in Custer's childhood and was further developed as he grew into adulthood. Custer was not accustomed to, nor did he place a high premium upon, doing things exactly by the book. This is not to say the boy general wasn't obedient to the commanders he served, because he was. But that desire to break free, to do things his way, was always just under the surface. Acting with a rash impunity during combat operations became commonplace with Custer, and it always drew the positive attention of his commanding officers and ensured that Custer would rise quickly in the ranks.

And because he was so exceedingly fortunate to have survived the perils of years of bloodshed, this mind-set (which received an inward stamp of approval because of his survival) only intensified once he sheathed his sword at the close of the Civil War. Viewing this in hindsight, it is easy to make a connection between the lack of parental discipline in his formative years and why he made such egregious mistakes in the last weeks of his life. As one writer has so astutely noted concerning Emanuel Custer and his ability to discipline his family: "His relationship to his sons seems to have been more that of an elder brother than of a traditional father. . . . Emanuel was anything but a disciplinarian. . . ."[7] Looking at young Custer's life through this particular lens will provide clues to the far-off disaster that made him immortal.

Without question, Maria was the more reserved of the two parents, and it appears that she provided whatever stability and order was found within the home. Somewhat sickly and frail, she was never a part of the horseplay that served as a bond between father and sons. Still, in many ways, she was the centerpiece of this loving, active, and very rambunctious family. And while Custer loved both parents deeply, it is without doubt that he revered and idolized his mother. Even after his marriage, Autie could be brought to tears upon hearing that his mother was distressed in any way.[8]

Another great influence on Custer was his half sister, Lydia Ann Kirkpatrick, who would become like a second mother to her energetic and high-spirited sibling. Custer never differentiated between half or full; to him they were all family. Lydia, some fourteen years older than Custer, had helped her mother raise their very large family and was especially close to her younger brother. And like Maria, she, too, wanted to provide a stable environment for Autie and would do her best to teach him what was important in life. The family would take advantage of this maternal instinct when, at the age of fourteen, Autie was relieved of his farm duties and sent to live with Lydia and her husband, David Reed, in Monroe, Michigan. They hoped to channel some of his boundless energy into a degree of academic success, which had eluded him to this point, more from a lack of application than any paucity of talent. Here he would enroll in Alfred Stebbins Young Men's Academy, where he would receive the best schooling Monroe, a town of some 3,500 people, had to offer.

This pattern of academic resistance—or rather, a refusal to apply oneself to the scholastic regimen required to consistently receive high marks—was still plaguing young Custer as he arrived at Stebbins. It's not that George wasn't eager to learn; he just wanted a curriculum of his own choosing. He had a habit of procuring from the school's library the latest books about famous military leaders or long-ago battles waged on the European continent and reading them in class. This task was always accomplished by hiding his current literary choice behind his much larger textbook. Indeed, he did this with such regularity that the entire class became aware of it, yet his teacher, who would often stroll up and down the aisles, never suspected a thing. George also shied away from doing homework and became adept at quickly memorizing the day's lesson before he was called upon to speak.[9] Here again, Mr. Stebbins never suspected young Custer of cutting such corners in his pursuit of an education. Overall, life at Stebbins was pleasant for George, and he would remain at the school until its closure two years later.

By the age of sixteen, Custer was back with the family on their farm on the outskirts of New Rumley. He had also by this time managed to acquire a certificate to actually teach others, and this he did first at Beach Point School in Athens, Ohio. Apparently, Custer started to mature mentally and emotionally at this time, as he began to apply himself in the area of preparing his students. The importance of a good education had started to take root within the young man, and Custer, the formerly mediocre student, was determined to become an exceptional teacher. Even so, academic mediocrity for Custer the student would continue to plague him later during his years at West Point.

Custer enrolled the following year at the McNeely Normal School in Hopedale, Ohio, to further his education. It would be around this time that Custer considered applying to the United States Military Academy at West Point. From all available evidence, his sole goal seemed to be that of furthering his education, for although Custer enjoyed reading about the military adventures of the soldiers of the day and was fascinated by the Ohio Militia his father was a part of, there is little to show that he had finalized his decision to pursue a military career. It was 1856, and seventeen-year-old George Armstrong Custer was about to take the largest step thus far to ensure his future as a warrior.

As his time at McNeely was coming to an end, Custer secured a teaching position at District Number Five, in Cadiz, Ohio, where he took a room with Alexander Holland and his family. But the living arrangements would prove to be anything but routine, as Custer and Holland's teenage daughter, Mollie, apparently fell madly in love. No one knows for sure if sex was a part of the relationship, although it seems likely that it was. It is a fact that when Alexander Holland learned that the two had been visiting on a "trundle bed," the schoolteacher was asked to leave.[10] Custer's banishment from his sweetheart (seemingly the first such emotional bonding for him, as well as for the girl) did not stop the two from corresponding, and Custer went so far as to invite the possibility of marriage while declaring his unbridled and everlasting love. Even so, this relationship would soon die on the vine as Custer went on with his life, and Mr. Holland's daughter did the same. For Custer, that meant chasing a much more elusive and harder-won prey: an appointment to West Point.

Just getting into West Point was no easy task. One had to be appointed by a state's congressman or senator, and once acceptance to the academy had become a reality, one had to overcome the very stringent and difficult entrance exam. But the exam was not even in the equation at this time for Custer. His greatest obstacle was just getting his foot in the door. The most obvious problem was that he was a Democrat in a largely Republican state. He was also the son of a well-known and rather caustic anti-Republican (rabid anti-Republican would be a more appropriate description), asking for help from Republican congressman John Bingham. But Custer, never one to run at the first sign of trouble, began contacting Bingham, making his case first by letter and then by personal contact.

Of course, one must assume that the still-teenage Custer did an admirable job presenting himself to such a distinguished figure, yet there may have been other aspects at play of which Custer was unaware. First, Bingham had already appointed one person to the Academy (only one person per congressional district could be appointed yearly, but because they were political appointments, there were sometimes ways around this limit), and was in contact with another young man who wanted the appointment. However, Bingham was also friends with Alexander Holland, and it is not outside the realm of possibility that Alexander, still reeling from whatever relationship Custer was having with his beloved daughter, very much wanted to see him far enough away so that their infatuation with one another would die a natural death. If arriving at this goal meant asking a favor of a friend, it's likely he did so.

Whatever happened, George Custer, as if riding on the backs of the stars as they raced into perfect alignment, received his wish to be part of a proud military tradition, and he was appointed to West Point. It was the first in a long series of fortuitous events that would occur in Custer's life—events the public was always quick to point to as an example of "Custer's Luck," and who could deny it?

Custer would enter the United States Military Academy at West Point little changed from the mischievous boy who had become so well known in the small hamlet of New Rumley and the little town of Monroe. Yet he was there, and while it remained to be seen what he would become or how long the young cadet could survive, he was at least at a profound crossroads, and he knew it. This was a defining moment for him; without it, his future would have been in question. Though he possessed the true heart of a warrior, Custer needed the Academy so that he would be "in place" once hostilities commenced. He was young, energetic, and almost completely without fear of any kind, and his country was going to need such men in the very dark and difficult years ahead.

Although unable to truly grasp the significance of the moment, Custer was ready to discard any semblance of civilian life in exchange for the life of a soldier. While he had given careful consideration to a career in education, his transition to a precarious life committed to armed conflict was assured the moment he put on the uniform of a military cadet. Though he had yet to realize his destiny, he was the type of person who was far happier making history than reading about it. Nor would he have been satisfied in the types of careers that most people find fulfilling and promise more than comfortable living. For young Custer, the road ahead would be paved with danger and physical deprivation. It would include the things he loved the most— a life on horseback and being outdoors in all types of weather, and the supreme adventure of surprising people at the moment they least expected it (a necessary element of a good prank, and later, of successful warfare). George Armstrong Custer was now in his true element. Everything prior to this moment had been merely obligatory preparation for the unusual life he was to lead. Each footstep he took was placing him that much closer to a destiny that would far exceed anything he could have imagined. He was a military icon in the making, and there was no stopping him.

Custer arrived at West Point in June of 1857. Like other schools and colleges, classes would not begin until late August, but entrance into West Point meant the obligatory summer encampment on the school's grounds. Housed in large, white military tents, the plebes would learn to quickly adapt to the full-time regimen of marching, drilling, and, above all else, relinquishing the identity of self for the oneness and cohesion of a military unit. These would be stringent years for Custer, and that summer encampment was just a foretaste of what was to come. It was the beginning of a molding that would last a lifetime. Even so, the boyishness of the young warrior would continue throughout his time here, and he would never garner the reputation of some of the previous attendees of the famed military academy.

West Point, situated some fifty miles north of New York City, sits atop high ground overlooking the Hudson River. Although the academy was founded in 1802, it had been an important garrison of the Continental Army since January of 1778. At that time, the British, having taken New York City two years earlier, were a constant and very real threat should they have decided to push northward. Both the Americans and the British understood the importance of the Hudson River as a tool in this war. Therefore, guarding the valuable S-turn in the river was of the utmost importance, as it was the best location from which to fire upon any flotilla of British gunboats or troopships trying to make their way north. Indeed, it was the most valuable piece of military real estate in the region, and the Continental Army made good use of it, planting stone-walled forts to welcome the red-coated soldiers of King George and stringing a massive, heavy iron chain from one side of the river to the other.

Sylvanus Thayer, known today as "the father of West Point," was a central figure in developing the academy as an institution of higher learning. Having been appointed superintendent by President James Monroe in 1817 (he would resign his position in 1833 after a falling-out with President Andrew Jackson), Thayer left his mark on West Point like no other. A scholar and a respected military man, Thayer was a veteran of the War of 1812, and was responsible for the implementation of a curriculum at West Point where mathematics and engineering played a leading role. Indeed, his academic footprint is still evident at the academy today.

Needless to say, by 1857 Custer was ensconced within an institution that offered the very best academic and military training in the country. The extensive military training at West Point (the very reason for its existence) was a joy to Custer, and held the greatest appeal for him. The classroom aspect of life at the Point, however, was a different story, and

Custer would barely be able to keep his head above water academically, regardless of the subject matter. That he was a mediocre student while at the academy was well known throughout the ranks, but it never seemed to trouble young Custer—or anyone else, for that matter. Surprisingly, he even managed to do poorly in the study of cavalry tactics, a subject in which one would automatically assume he would have done well. Yet even here, if the knowledge was to be gained from a book or from the mouth of a professor, Custer's inner drive to excel in areas of military learning was not present. All of this held little significance for him when compared to the actual hands-on preparation for the battlefield. Thus, Custer's years at West Point would be marked by an exceedingly poor academic showing. It was simply of no importance to him to rise to the level where his scholastic achievements would stand above those of his peers. And so, as this very unique individual and soldier approached graduation that spring of 1861, he was about to capture the inglorious distinction of graduating thirty-fourth in a class of thirty-four.

Not surprisingly, the boyish antics of Custer's youth would be with him throughout his years at the academy, and his cavalier attitude ensured that he racked up demerits on a regular basis. It would be these disciplinary marks that would, at different times, bring him very close to expulsion. It mattered little to his superiors that demerits were levied against cadets for even the most minor offenses, such as tardiness, a slightly wrinkled uniform, throwing snowballs, playing cards, or even a messy room. Any infraction of the myriad West Point rules produced an immediate backlash against the wayward cadet. As such, a total of more than one hundred demerits in any one semester meant automatic dismissal. And on two occasions, Custer came very close to packing his bags, racking up a whopping ninety-four and ninety-eight demerits, respectively. There is little evidence that Custer was overly troubled by this (except when he was nearly expelled), and his good-natured rebelliousness at the Point served him well with his admiring peers.

Even so, one particular incident just prior to graduation illustrates perfectly Custer's penchant for going his own way, at his own peril, and breaking the rules whenever he deemed it necessary. Writing in the 1874 issue of *Galaxy* magazine, Custer, now with perfect hindsight, describes the events that so exemplified his nature: "It so happened that it fell to my detail to perform the duties of officer of the guard in camp, at a time when the arrival of the order from Washington officially transforming us from cadets to officers was daily expected."[11] Throughout that day, Custer handled himself well, and it wasn't until dusk that the soon-to-be officer came upon two cadets embroiled in an argument that was about to turn physical. His only duty at this point was to exercise his authority and quell the escalating disturbance. Within seconds, however, the two started pounding each other with their fists, and while some cadets rushed forward to break up the fight, Custer's immature and impulsive nature rose to the occasion. Instead of stopping the fight and arresting the pair, he gave his official endorsement. Looking back on the incident, Custer remarked, ". . . the instincts of the boy prevailed over the obligation of the officer of the guard. I pushed my way through the surrounding line of cadets, dashed back those who were interfering in the struggle, and called out loudly, 'Stand back, boys; let's have a fair fight.'"[12] Fair, perhaps, but very unwise. Within seconds of this, two officers were spotted approaching, and the observing crowd of cadets quickly ran away. Custer, already regretting his rash decision, ran for the officer of the guard tent, hoping to escape the notice of the officers. It made little difference, as he'd already been identified by the two, and soon he was called before Lieutenant-Colonel John F. Reynolds, who placed Custer under arrest and ordered him to return to his tent.

Within hours of his being placed under house arrest, the expected orders came through. Everyone but Custer was now officially exchanging their cadet uniform for that of a US Army officer. War was igniting with the South, and Custer, who had graduated last in his class but was destined to become the most famous among them, could do nothing but wait for the anticipated punishment. Thankfully, not only was he needed for the combat soon to come, but Custer also had numerous friends who were willing to contact the right individuals who could help. At his court-martial, Custer received the proverbial slap on the wrist (a written reprimand), and was dispatched to Washington, D.C.

Arriving in New York City en route to Washington, Custer stopped at Horstmann's, a military outfitter, for "saber, revolver, sash, spurs, etc."[13] It is clear the excitement of war had gripped the nation. The train carrying Custer to Washington was packed with troops. At each stop, Custer related, ". . . crowds of citizens were assembled [and] provided bountifully with refreshments, which they distributed in the most lavish manner among the troops. . . . It was no unusual sight, on leaving a station surrounded by these loyal people, to see matrons and maidens embracing and kissing with patriotic fervor the men, entire strangers to them, whom they saw hastening to the defense of the nation."[14]

The moment had arrived. His years of preparation were now over. This train ride south was Custer's entrance to his life as a warrior, and the "myth" of what he would ultimately become was already taking shape. All of those young men, clad in dark blue uniforms, would soon undergo their own personal baptism of fire. A war unlike anything they could have imagined was beginning to take shape, and it would claim hundreds of thousands of lives on both sides. For many involved, it would spark internal horror, abject fear, and a sense of dread. But for George Armstrong Custer, it was like going home, or being introduced to a lifelong friend. He was finally in his element—except here, the element was as cold as steel. It would be here, among the booming of cannon and the screams of the wounded, that George Custer would claim his rightful place. Once discovered, this realm of violence would remain preeminent, ascending in importance over all other aspects of life. War would be like a mistress to Custer, and he would always be faithful to her, until death itself released him from her iron grip.

CHAPTER 2

Blood and Glory

In the summer of 1861, Washington, D.C., was in a state of continual upheaval and preparation for the impending war. When the rebels bombarded Fort Sumter in early April of 1861, it was clear that hostilities had reached the point of no return, and President Lincoln ordered the defenses of the city to be strengthened. He understood that the capital was going to be the jumping-off point for the start of this war—the citizens were already clamoring for the army to march on Richmond—but it was a target for the Confederates as well. As such, the only fortified defense the city could look to for protection was Fort Washington, located along the Potomac River some twelve miles south of the city. But even this would mean little once a concentrated attack on Washington occurred. By August 17, however, General George McClellan had taken charge, placing forts, batteries of field artillery, and interconnecting entrenchments for riflemen, all of which would have a devastating effect on the attackers.[1] By war's end, Washington was impregnable against attack, having some ninety forts ringing the city, with twenty miles of rifle pits and ninety-three batteries of field artillery that could be unleashed at a moment's notice.[2]

At this time there was a palpable sense of urgency, as regular army and volunteer units consisting of infantry and artillery began streaming into the city. Lincoln was well aware that the rebels, under the command of Brigadier General Pierre G. T. Beauregard, were assembling their forces just a few miles south, and it was only a matter of time before a major battle erupted. Lincoln's pick to destroy Beauregard's army was Brigadier

General Irvin McDowell, recently appointed as commander of the Army of Northeastern Virginia. Naturally, both armies were untested in battle, and McDowell's fears concerning the capability of his troops to succeed in war were perhaps laid to rest by a comment from the president himself: "You are green, it is true," Lincoln reminded him, "but they are green also; you are all green alike."[3] And while many a voice could be heard clamoring for the North to strike a decisive blow (something Lincoln wanted very much to do) and begin a march on Richmond, they were in no real position to do so. As they would soon learn, the longer a fight could be averted, the better off Washington would be.

Custer arrived in the capital on July 20. Grabbing his gear, Custer stepped off the train and made his way to Ebbitt House, where, as Custer remembered it, "I expected to find some of my classmates domiciled." Custer did find a number of friends there, including his closest from West Point, James P. Parker, from Missouri. However, the meeting was bittersweet, as Custer soon learned that like so many other Southern friends and classmates from the Point, Parker was going to fight under the flag of rebellion. "He was one of the few members of my class," Custer wrote, "who, while sympathizing with the South, had remained at the Academy long enough to graduate and secure a diploma." Because Custer had arrived so early, he found Parker in bed. After discussing the gathering of armies for battle, Custer asked his friend about his immediate plans. Without rising from bed, Parker told him to look over a document on a nearby table. It was from the War Department, "dismissing from the rolls of the army Second Lieutenant James P. Parker, for having tendered his resignation in the face of the enemy."[4] Parker would be fighting under the Rebel flag. Custer bid his friend a sad farewell.

The next day, the first Battle of Bull Run would begin, just a few miles outside of Washington, near Manassas, Virginia (Southern forces referred to this battle as First Manassas). Custer would see very little of the bloodletting. Acting as a courier for General Winfield Scott, Custer's mission was to deliver orders to General McDowell's headquarters, located in Centerville, Virginia. (McDowell's nemesis, General Beauregard, was plotting the Union commander's destruction at Manassas Junction, some seven miles away.) Custer arrived in Centerville, the very epicenter of the Union Army, just prior to 3:00 a.m. The troops, already up and moving, were ready to begin the day's march, as it was McDowell's intention to crush the Rebel forces in a matter of hours. But a delay in orders meant the men, fully equipped, were lining both sides of the road, and by the time Custer rode up, many of the soldiers had stretched out on the ground in an attempt to catch more sleep. Custer had to take great care so that his horse wouldn't trample any unsuspecting men. When Custer located the headquarters of General McDowell, he intended to deliver the orders personally, but he was prevented from doing so by one of McDowell's attending officers. This didn't sit well with Custer, but there was nothing else he could do. He was pleased to see an old friend from the academy, and soon the two were sharing conversation over breakfast while Custer's horse was being fed and cared for.

Spread out to the west and southwest, another force of some thirty thousand soldiers was also up and moving for the day, and they too had plans for battle. Indeed, a major clash was becoming inevitable, as you cannot have two large armies in such close proximity, trying to outflank, probe for weaknesses, and dance around each other for very long, without making contact. Still, beyond a skirmish or two, nothing of significance had yet happened.

Having rested, Custer made his way through a throng of infantry to where the Second Cavalry was waiting for orders to move, and it wasn't long before the crackling of rifles and the booming of cannon could be heard in the distance. As daylight spread across the land, it brought with it the certainty of contact. At approximately 10:00 a.m., scores of Union troops began fording Bull Run Creek, pressing the attack. The battle would rage for the next five or so hours. For a while, McDowell's troops had the upper hand, but the tide of battle was about to turn.

Because Custer's cavalry unit was purposely held back, the men were forced to play a waiting game. The sights and sounds of battle were all around them, yet Custer's baptism of fire, albeit a relatively gentle one when compared to the bloody work of the infantry units that day, was even then unfolding. Sitting in the saddle, Custer watched artillery burst in the sky, sending shards of iron into nearby trees. He heard, for the first time, the strange hissing sound that solid cannonballs make as they split the air overhead, and watched occasional bursts of shells as they tore holes in the ground to his left or right.[5] Soon, he would become part of the now-famous retreat as an attack by Confederate forces quickly got the upper hand. Once the momentum was in their favor, it quickly became a rout.

Such an action must have gnawed at Custer a bit, for *retreat* was not a word in his vocabulary. Describing in almost humorous terms the condition of the troops on that first day of war, he writes: "The long lines of Union soldiery, which a few minutes before had been bravely confronting and driving the enemy, suddenly lost their cohesion and became one immense mass of fleeing, frightened creatures. Artillery horses were cut from their traces, and it was no unusual sight to see three men, perhaps belonging to different regiments, riding the same horse, and making their way to the rear as fast as the dense mass of men moving with them would permit. . . . An occasional shot from the enemy's artillery, or the cry that the Black Horse cavalry, so dreaded in the first months of the war in Virginia, were coming, kept the fleeing crowd of soldiers at their best speed."[6]

Speaking of the weapons, flags, and musical equipment littering the ground, Custer also referred to the hysterical troopers as "flying Federals,"[7] and related how one regiment, the Zouaves, kept retreating, passing through Washington, D.C., and refusing to stop until they were safely in New York.[8] Custer's cavalry unit was the last organized body of troops to leave the field. Centerville, a town that had seemed so solidly in Union hands only hours before when Custer had ridden through it, was now a sea of gray uniforms, and would remain so for some time to come.

In all, the fight was fairly evenly split, with approximately 18,000 troops on each side taking part in the battle. As the sun receded in the western sky, without question, it had not been a good first day for Mr. Lincoln's Army, but at least the real war had commenced, and for that, the president was thankful. Northern dead were listed at 406, with over 1,100 wounded. The Confederates lost 387, with almost 1,600 wounded. But these casualty figures were nothing in comparison to what was coming. The final "causality" of the battle was McDowell himself, who was relieved of command. Lincoln's pick to replace the disgraced commander was George McClellan, thirty-four years old and from a well-to-do Philadelphia family.

As a boy of thirteen, McClellan was already attending the University of Pennsylvania for the study of law. Two years later, however, he changed his mind and decided to become a soldier. With the assistance of his father, who promptly wrote a letter to President John Tyler, the studious youngster entered West Point Military Academy. Unlike Custer, McClellan was a good student, and upon graduation in 1846, took second place in a class of fifty-nine.[9] Also unlike Custer (and as Lincoln would discover), McClellan was sadly lacking the internal qualities necessary to function as a warrior. Preparation at the academy to become a soldier does not necessarily make one an effective and competent combat leader. McClellan was not the man for the job, as the president would soon discover.

In March of 1862, Custer and the Fifth Cavalry became part of a great flotilla of 120,000 men, 15,000 horses, and arms heading south by boats, steamers, barges, and anything else suitable for transporting an army for this better-late-than-never campaign launched by the reticent George B. McClellan. It was a bold move to capture Richmond, and had another commander been at the helm, victory may have been achieved. But the timidity which had engulfed McClellan earlier, causing him to reject the idea (and the suggestions of the president) of attacking the fortified Confederates at Manassas, would sail with him to Fort Monroe, and would ultimately lead to defeat there as well.

Moving south, this massive war machine sailed down Chesapeake Bay, disembarking at Fort Monroe, located at the tip of the peninsula. Prior to their arrival, the Union Navy had secured the area by a blockade, dubbed Anaconda, but not before the loss of two ships (one sunk and one run aground), courtesy of the Confederate ironclad warship, the CSS

Virginia. Thus began what is known as the Peninsula Campaign. Up until this point, Custer's war experience had been spotty at best, but now began a phase of protracted combat for all involved. They were now striking at the heart of the Confederacy, and contact with the Rebels came quickly. A slugfest was about to begin.

The peninsula is flanked by the York and James Rivers. The Union Army, inching northward, encountered fortifications within twenty miles of their base camp at Fort Monroe, and indeed, the Rebels had lines of defense from this point to Yorktown, approximately twelve miles to the east. The Confederate defenses at this point were relatively weak, consisting only of General John "the Prince" Magruder's 1,300-man army, a force that would not be able to sustain an attack such as McClellan could launch, should he decide to do so. Unable to add reinforcements quickly to this potential battlefield, Magruder, an amateur actor with a clear understanding of how to properly stage a scene, began marching his troops around, moving men and equipment up and down the line, giving the impression of a much larger force. The ploy worked, and McClellan's superior numbers came to a grinding halt. This move would allow time for an additional 38,000 troops under the command of General Joseph Johnston to arrive and bolster the Rebel forces. Had McClellan attacked when he had first encountered the enemy, he would have smashed through their lines as if swatting at a fly. Instead, the timid commander began a siege where one was unnecessary, carving out his own fortifications and emplacing large siege mortars before Yorktown. In a letter to General Robert E. Lee, Johnston, understanding the dire circumstances Magruder faced upon McClellan's arrival, perfectly summed up the benefits of facing such an enemy: "No one but McClellan could have hesitated to attack."[10] Confederate General James Longstreet, just about as able an opponent McClellan or the North could face, would later write how "[McClellan] was not quick or forcible in handling his troops."[11]

Custer's Peninsula war began rather slowly. In a letter to his sister, Lydia, Custer tells of their encounter with the enemy along Warwick Stream: "Our army is encamped in front of the rebels. We are getting ready for the expected battle. Our troops are building batteries right under their fortifications. . . . I was in the woods with our sharpshooters. . . . Everyone got behind a tree and blazed away as hard as he could. But the rebels made their bullets fly so thick it was all we could do to look out for ourselves. . . . This was before our troops had thrown up breast-works."[12] But Custer's "expected battle" would not materialize, at least on the current front, and the "siege" of Yorktown would end with a whimper when the Confederates abandoned their trenches on May 3. Had General Johnston not pulled his men from the line when he did, they most assuredly would have suffered extensive casualties from the siege mortars lobbing hundreds of shells, some of which weighed two hundred pounds. So, not only had the Confederates outsmarted McClellan at the beginning (which produced the "siege" in the first place), but they had also slipped away before the first shot of this major bombardment could be fired. President Lincoln's frustration continued. The Federals, however, would finally move, and the first major event of the Peninsula Campaign would unfold at Williamsburg.

It is of interest to note that during the Siege of Yorktown, Custer was used as an observer in a balloon. This afforded him an excellent view of the Confederate lines and their activities. It is also clear from his writing that being a thousand feet in the air was something he had never envisioned. "[T]he proposed ride was far more elevated than I had ever desired or contemplated," he wrote. "It was a kind of danger that few persons have schooled themselves against, and still fewer possess a liking for."[13] Even so, Custer would be the first to discover the nocturnal departure of the enemy: "Upon the evening of the 3rd of May the division commander directed me to make two ascensions during the night, one immediately after dark, the other just before reveille."[14] During his first trip into the night sky, nothing unusual was observed; however, during his second trip aloft, he could clearly see fires and explosions in the area of Williamsburg, followed by the delayed sound of the blasts. He also observed the many fires springing up along Union lines, denoting the making of coffee and breakfast of the Army of the Potomac. No such activity could be observed from the Confederate entrenchments, and as morning fully developed, McClellan knew the reason why. His desire to pound the Rebels into submission was not to be fulfilled.

The clash at Williamsburg on May 5 (there had been at least two cavalry fights the day before), or more appropriately, the battle at Fort Magruder and its smaller earthen fortifications fronting Williamsburg, would be both bloody and inconclusive. It would not, as McClellan hoped, do anything to stop the organized fighting retreat of Rebel forces toward Richmond. Without realizing it, McClellan had missed an opportunity that was still viable, and the Confederates were taking full advantage of his mistake. Comprising some 41,000 Union troops and nearly 32,000 Confederates, it was the first major engagement of the Peninsula Campaign. The fight brought unexpected surprises to both sides, as all battles have a tendency to take on a life of their own despite the planning or attention of the opposing commanders. One Confederate counterattack produced the lopsided statistic of over 800 Rebel casualties to the Union's 100. Even so, the final tally of dead and wounded would be as follows: Union losses stood at 2,283, with 1,682 for the Rebels. Custer, who had requested a temporary assignment to General Hancock's brigade to participate in the fight, notes that it was here they first heard the famous Rebel yell.[15]

And so the race northward began, the Rebels trying to fight a successful retreat and to fortify Richmond before McClellan could bring his army to bear in their own backyard. McClellan, desiring to smash the Rebels before they could reach their stronghold, sent troops up the York River in hopes of cutting them off. But a bold attack by the cavalry of General John Bell Hood on May 7 stopped them in their tracks. On May 15, Union gunboats steamed up the James River, probing the Confederate defenses, but were turned back by a pounding from Rebel cannon atop Drewry's Bluff. So far, things were not going well for the Federals. Indeed, as McClellan approached Richmond with some 105,000 troops, he believed the enemy possessed a superior number, when in fact their force totaled only 60,000. Once again, McClellan would stage a siege, this time just short of Richmond itself, the very heart of the Confederacy. Of course, there wasn't any way the Rebel leadership was going to allow the city of Richmond to be reduced to a pile of rubble by McClellan's siege guns, so a counterattack was in their future.

On May 24, 1862, Custer's star began its first ascent, when, according to a topographical engineer, Lieutenant Bowen, Custer waded, pistol in hand, into the Chickahominy River to gauge its depth. According to Bowen, "Lieutenant Custer, Fifth US Cavalry . . . was the first to cross the stream, the first to open fire on the enemy, and one of the last to leave the field."[16] Indeed, had there been a sharp-eyed Rebel sentry watching for such an unlikely event, he could have taken aim and cut short the life of this bold young cavalry officer. This event, fortuitous beyond Custer's imagination, brought him into the presence of General McClellan himself, a man he absolutely worshipped.

Writing home, Custer told his family: "I have more confidence in General McClellan than in any man living. I would forsake everything and follow him to the ends of the earth. I would lay down my life for him. . . . Every officer and private worships him. I would fight anyone who would say a word against him."[17] Of course, Custer had been a witness to McClellan's glaring mistakes during the Peninsula Campaign, but his endless respect for the man kept him from grasping the true nature of his folly. In any event, Custer found it impossible to decline McClellan's offer to act as his aide-de-camp. With it came a promotion to the rank of captain.

On May 27, Union and Confederate forces clashed at Hanover Courthouse, with inconclusive results. But on May 31, and lasting until June 1, the Battle of Seven Pines (referred to as Fair Oaks by the Union troops) changed the entire course of the campaign in the Confederates' favor. At this time, McClellan's army was split by the Chickahominy River, with two-thirds of his troops south of the river (and closest to the Rebels), and one-third on the other side. It was General Johnston's intention to strike at McClellan's army and smash it before it could be reinforced, driving him back down the peninsula. It was a good plan, although impossible to execute without numerous logistical mistakes (not an unusual occurrence when attempting to move large bodies of troops around). The attack apparently shocked McClellan and effectively stopped him from continuing his plans to bring Richmond to its knees. Johnston would be wounded twice during the battle, almost simultaneously, on the second day of fighting when he was hit in the shoulder and chest by a bullet and shell fragment. Unable to lead his men while recuperating, Johnston's command was taken over by General Robert E. Lee on the order of President Jefferson Davis, and that meant a veritable lion had been unleashed upon McClellan. This appointment would be decisive for the South.

What Lee unleashed on the Yankees was a turning of the tables, and now they were forced to endure their own fighting retreat back down the peninsula. Casualties would be high on both sides in what is known as the Seven Days Battles, with Confederate dead and wounded (20,204) exceeding Northern losses (15,855). Those who survived the horrendous fighting would never forget the names attached to the sites of slaughter: Mechanicsville (Beaver Dam Creek), Gaines's Mill, Savage's Station, Glendale, White Oak Swamp, and Malvern Hill. This was a period of sustained bloodletting, and George Custer was in the thick of it. Indeed, it would be during the fighting at White Oak Swamp that Custer would deal a death blow to a Confederate officer who refused to surrender, an act for which he would be unfairly judged by some.[18]

Having charged a Rebel gun emplacement near White Oak Swamp—which immediately broke and ran—Custer, on the heels of a fleeing Confederate, shouted a command for the man to surrender. When Custer heard no response, he shouted out the command to surrender once more, but this, too, was in vain. Custer fired his pistol at him but missed. A second shot found its mark, knocking the gray-clad officer from his saddle. Custer was galloping so quickly that he flew past the crumpled form upon the ground and could not see what happened next. According to Lieutenant Byrnes, the mortally wounded Rebel ". . . rose to his feet, turned around, threw up his hands, and fell to the ground with a stream of blood gushing from his mouth."[19]

Because Custer had described the horse that carried the officer as "splendid," and because he chose to shoot the man instead of the horse, this is given as proof of his callousness. Never mind that it was the man who presented the danger to Custer and not the horse. One thing is certain: When the fleeing officer ignored Custer's order to stop, a violent end was assured. Writing later of the incident, Custer put the responsibility squarely on the Rebel officer, who obviously desired to escape so he might fight another day. Being wounded evidently changed his plans, but the bullet had struck a vital area, and death—not surrender—was now only seconds away. That Custer would later describe this encounter as if it had been an exciting hunt means absolutely nothing. Veterans have been doing this for as long as there have been wars. After all, in Custer's mind, it was more than a mere contest, seeing that he had offered his opponent the chance to surrender. Custer's decision to extend this mercy could have easily resulted in his own death.

Callousness *did* exist within the heart of George Custer, but it was not directed at any particular individual, nor could it be defined by any one particular incident. His insensitivity could be attributed to the emotional detachment that comes from the battlefield, where Custer himself could have died. The harsh price that is paid by those who participate in war simply did not bother him. Instead of fearing his own end, Custer became emotionally attached to that activity which offered death at every turn. As his personal letters revealed, Custer found pleasure in the sights and sounds of combat, referring to cavalry charges as "beautiful" and "glorious."[20] After one particular charge the young warrior confessed that he never expected to see a "prettier sight."[21] He also spoke of enjoying seeing "the glittering sabres advance in the sunlight."[22] It never mattered that these same glittering weapons would soon be hacking away at human flesh, severing arteries, nerves, and families forever. Custer was very much unashamed when it came to his love for war, and admitted as much to a cousin, writing in a letter that, as far as he was concerned, "I must say that I shall regret to see the war end. I would be willing, yes, glad, to see a battle every day of my life."[23] He did, however, quickly express a change of heart when considering the pain and grief the war had caused others: "I cannot but earnestly hope for peace, and at an early date."[24] His cousin understood that Custer loved battle. He loved the hunt and the chase of war. He loved exposing himself to danger, no matter how heavy the combat or precarious the situation. And yes, he enjoyed the "kill," for that is the end result of the love of war. Without the destruction of your opponent, war is little more than a children's game.

Custer's bravery under fire was nothing short of legendary. Always at the head of his men, he would charge into battle with an intensity that would stay constant throughout his life. If he ever experienced fear while on the battlefield, it must have been minimal, and certainly not the paralyzing type of fear or dread that can keep one from performing one's duties. Such zeal in battle often leads to extinction, of course, but in Custer's case, it was always the man beside him, or behind him, who was sent reeling into oblivion. And while Custer was indeed a skilled cavalryman, in such heated hand-to-hand contests, skill will only take you so far, ultimately guaranteeing you nothing. Here, the brave, the cowardly, the swift, and the slow can all die together. As the corpses piled up, privates and generals alike, Custer was never among them.

It was also very important for Custer to have officers surrounding him who were of like nature. Writing a letter to the young woman his friend, Captain Jacob Greene, was seeing, Custer explained how he took him to a place where the Rebel bullets were coming in "thick and fast." Obviously watching him closely for any sign of fear, Custer was pleased to report that Greene "never faltered, was as calm and collected as if sitting at dinner."[25]

——————

Malvern Hill, a fortified Yankee stronghold close to the James River, was Custer's last major battle in the Union's retreat back down the peninsula. On July 1, the Confederate Army was determined to keep the pressure on McClellan, perhaps defeating him once and for all. It turned out to be an exceedingly bad idea, as Rebel casualties mounted quickly under a heavy and sustained cannonading by numerous Federal batteries, in what may have been the most intense bombardment of the war. Southern losses at day's end would be 5,300 to the Union's 3,200—a clear victory for the North, as the South gained nothing in the attack. Even so, the ever-timid McClellan never considered that a counteroffensive was warranted. Still believing his forces were greatly outnumbered, he chose to do nothing, and continued his push toward home. George Custer would live to fight another day.

CHAPTER 3

Love in a Time of War

The year 1862 had been a busy and adventurous one for Custer. Indeed, there had been time for little else but war and the uncertainties of battle. But Custer's world was about to include the love of a woman. The romance that would blossom between George Armstrong Custer and Elizabeth Bacon would surpass any previous love interest the young warrior had ever experienced. Libbie, as she would become known to the world, was the daughter of Judge Daniel S. Bacon, a prominent figure among the upper class in Monroe, Michigan, of which Custer was not a part. It would be this societal gulf, and the prejudicial nature of Daniel Bacon, that would keep the judge in a state of perpetual disapproval when it came to Custer and Libbie becoming a couple. Yet there was a second hurdle Custer would have to face, as the judge didn't want his daughter to marry *any* soldier, lest she become a widow before she had time to become a wife. For the young warrior, winning over the judge in this or any area became just another battle to be fought, and he was more than up to the task.

Ironically, Custer and Libbie had "met" once, in 1861, when a fairly inebriated Custer, on leave visiting his sister, went weaving on foot past the Bacon home in Monroe. Needless to say, it did not cause Libbie to view the young cavalry officer, no matter how dashing he may have looked in his Union blues, as anything special; Libbie even referred to this incident as "that awful day."[1] Yet they were destined to meet again, and Custer, having permanently sworn off the bottle, would make a far better impression this time around. Interestingly, Libbie's father also had a chance to meet Custer during that trip home, producing a quick public handshake between a young soldier and a well-respected member of Monroe's community.

In September 1862, Custer fought in what turned out to be the bloodiest day of the war, at Antietam, Maryland. Soon after this, he came down with an illness and was granted an extended leave. Naturally, he came home to Monroe. While at home, a most fortuitous event occurred: He was invited to a Thanksgiving party at Boyd's Seminary, an exclusive school for girls in Monroe. Hosted by the principals, Erasmus J. and Sarah Boyd, it was a defining moment for the two, but it would not be love at first sight—at least not for twenty-two-year-old Libbie Bacon. None of that mattered to Custer, who was determined they would be together. He decided that he would pursue her until her emotions caught up with his. Just as he never considered defeat on the battlefield, he wouldn't be defeated here either. Indeed, the feelings of invincibility which pervaded his life (and always seemed to produce the proper results for Custer) would not be proven incorrect for another fourteen years. And in the case of Libbie, it wasn't long before Custer's constant romancing started to have a real effect on this Monroe socialite, and she began to view his attentiveness as a true sign of his love for her.

One aspect of the relationship worth mentioning is the opposite natures of these two people: While George Custer was as fearless a person as you'd ever hope to find, Libbie battled fear constantly. She was not so paralyzed by these sensations of fear and dread that she could not conduct her life (and in fact, one of her fears would be proven horribly correct on one occasion), but it was certainly an insidious companion for a good part of her life, and no doubt originated with the death of her mother when she was only twelve. It was never a point of contention between the two, and Custer must have realized that, in his chosen profession, it was only natural for the party who remained behind the scenes of such dangerous work to have bouts of apprehension. How could it be otherwise?

For a time, their courtship had to be kept a carefully guarded secret, as her father did not (and in Libbie's mind, would never) approve of the union. Of course, keeping it a secret from her father would work for only so long in a town as small as Monroe. But in time, as Custer racked up victories in battle that were clearly making a name for him, both on and off the battlefield, Daniel Bacon's outwardly gruff exterior began to soften. He warmed to the young cavalry officer who sported the long, blond locks, to the point where the judge began to inwardly consider the possibilities. Part of the father's reservations clearly rested in the concern that his only child (of the four born to the judge and Mrs. Bacon, only Libbie survived) would be devastated should Custer die in the war—not an unreasonable thought. Heartbreak, seemingly the order of the day for so many families of that time, had made an indelible impression on Daniel Bacon, and he approached the issue from this perspective.

So it was with great joy that Custer received a letter from Bacon welcoming the union between him and his daughter. It was a message which no doubt surprised Custer, as it was a complete about-face from what had appeared to be an implacable stand. Yet there he was, reading the words that guaranteed his future with the woman he loved above all others: "Pressed in the matter, and having learned from my daughter how much her happiness is really interested in you, I yield at last," Bacon wrote. "I consent to the marriage, and would be proud to welcome you as my son-in-law."[2] The judge, having watched Custer rise from a little-known cavalry captain on McClellan's staff to a seasoned war veteran whose name and exploits were becoming well known to a fascinated public, was starting to take notice of the young man. And, as if to top things off, on June 28, 1863, Custer became, at the age of twenty-three, the youngest brigadier general in the history of the nation, and only days later participated in the momentous Battle of Gettysburg, where he defeated the likes of Jeb Stuart and his battle-hardened cavalrymen known as the Invincibles. It was an amazing feat by the youthful warrior, and there was little else to be said. Judge Bacon relented and welcomed George Custer into the fold. After all, Daniel Bacon rightly reasoned, referring to such a man as his son-in-law would be a respectable thing, especially after Gettysburg made Custer a hero—not just in the eyes of himself, but throughout the country. As such, Custer's actions at Gettysburg are worthy of a closer look.

⌐ ∙ ⌐

On July 3, as men were dying (or about to die) in the infantry assaults around Gettysburg—including the horrendous slaughter for the South known as Pickett's Charge—a cavalry battle with a surprising ending was about to unfold several miles east of town.

James Ewell Brown (J. E. B.) Stuart, a brilliant cavalry commander, was considered to be the eyes and ears of Robert E. Lee for his ability to obtain accurate intelligence about the enemy's whereabouts and intentions. Stuart was determined to strike at the Federals' rear on that decisive day by smashing General Meade's forces, thereby assisting Pickett in his advance. Very adept at striking the Army of the Potomac at will, Stuart, commanding his Invincibles, had every reason to believe his plan of attack would come off beautifully. But here again, fate, chance, and the unexpected tide of battle would be dealing the cards, and the star of George Armstrong Custer would ascend even higher in history.

Personally leading numerous charges that afternoon, Custer's first dash toward the enemy almost became his last. Deciding to lead Company A of the Sixth Michigan Cavalry (generals do not lead single companies, but Custer just couldn't help himself), sixty strong, he attacked what they believed to be a rather insignificant number of Rebel skirmishers, a number that Custer thought did not exceed two hundred. This initial group did break into a retreat, but within moments, the jubilant Company A, with Custer at the point, was met by six hundred Confederates, the entire brigade of General Wade Hampton. Ready and waiting, the crack of hundreds of carbines greeted the Union attackers, and Custer's horse collapsed, sending him hurtling to the ground. Just as he was attempting to grab the arm of a trooper trying to pull him up on his horse, a Rebel took careful aim at Custer but was killed before he could pull the trigger. Hampton's men were not willing to merely wave good-bye to their startled foe, but pursued them as they retreated. In reality, it was more

32

like a gauntlet, but Custer's Luck had spared him once again. Company A suffered a casualty rate of 50 percent before Hampton's brigade was driven off by Custer's artilleryman, Alexander Pennington, whose guns sent out hot blasts of iron to meet the attackers.

Throughout the day, the cavalry divisions clashed. What a sight it must have presented as hordes of gray and blue slashed at each other in close combat, firing pistols at point-blank range, tumbling out of saddles, all in the midst of the smoke and dust of battle. During one charge, Custer raised his saber and yelled "Come on, you Wolverines!" leading his troopers in a dash across Rummel Farm, where dismounted Rebels began to break and run. At this point, killing and capturing the enemy was the natural result of this momentum, but as they reached a small rise, the galloping cavalrymen found themselves crashing into a low stone wall, with rail fencing fixed atop. Needless to say, they were followed by other surprised horsemen whose mounts careened into the mix of startled and wounded horses and men. The Confederates, seeing their advantage, started pouring rounds into them from just a short distance away. Many Rebels quickly ran and took up positions on the other side of the stone wall, and the firing at this point was so close that some recipients of the volley no doubt also sustained burns from the initial blast.[3] Within a short time the fencing was cleared, and Custer's "Wolverines" resumed the chase. Despite the reinforcing of his beleaguered troops, Stuart could not win the day. He was even then being defeated and outmaneuvered by George Custer.

Less than a year later, on May 11, 1864, Stuart would receive a mortal wound during the fighting at Yellow Tavern (also a Custer engagement), when a dismounted Yankee, forty-eight-year-old Private John A. Huff, took careful aim and fired his .44 caliber revolver at the Southern officer, hitting him in the side. The bullet exited his back and an iconic figure tumbled from his saddle. Stuart died from his wound the next day and was buried in Richmond's Hollywood Cemetery. Losing J. E. B. Stuart was a great loss to the Confederate Cavalry, and a personal loss to Robert E. Lee.

Custer again found himself in Monroe in the fall of 1863, recuperating from a shell-fragment wound in the thigh received during the fighting at Culpeper Courthouse, Virginia. It wasn't a serious wound, but it was enough to bring him home to his Libbie for a while, a welcome result. He had thus far come through some of the most ferocious fighting of the war with little damage to his body to show for it, and absolutely no impairment to his mind. On one occasion a Confederate bullet nearly ended the career of the boy general by clipping off a lock of his hair. During another fight he was hit twice, but the bullets, having lost nearly all their power, caused only minor bruises and swelling.[4] Ironically, the luck which had carried Custer safely in and out of battle would not extend to the beasts supporting him. During the fighting at Gettysburg in July of 1863, Custer lost three horses while engaging Robert E. Lee's Army of Northern Virginia. On another occasion, two of these very large targets crumpled under him within the span of only fifteen minutes.[5]

On February 9, 1864, while the ebb and flow of two vast armies in conflict were leaving thousands of dead and wounded scattered across the land, George Armstrong Custer and Elizabeth Clift Bacon became husband and wife. It was a marriage that would only last twelve years, cut short by Custer's untimely death. During this time Libbie would do everything possible to be as close to her husband as military authorities would allow. Leaving Monroe, Libbie would, like other army officer wives, be ensconced in Washington, D.C., where she would anxiously await the return of a husband who was almost constantly enveloped in the horrors of war. She would, however, do something many wives were either unwilling or unable to do: Discarding the comforts of the nation's capital, whenever possible Libbie Custer would join her husband at his various military camps. They were very often muddy, hectic, loud, and lacking the refinement she was accustomed to; Libbie Custer nevertheless considered it a fair trade. Indeed, her desire to be close to her Autie would lead her to places she'd only read about and never expected to visit. Whatever road they were on throughout their life, she must have reasoned, they would be on it together.

The battles and skirmishes of 1864 would be bloody and without letup until the agonizing end. Bleeding the South of men and material in an effort to preserve the Union had been exceedingly costly, and those still able-bodied individuals like Custer who participated in so much of the war, year after bloody year, could forever consider themselves extremely lucky. Indeed, the largest cavalry clash of the war, the Battle of Trevilian Station, unfolded in early June of 1864, and Custer would find himself not just in the thick of it, but displaying the type of military leadership that was so unique to his character. And just as at Little Bighorn some twelve years later, Custer would find himself almost completely surrounded.

In what was part of General Grant's Overland Campaign, consisting of battles now etched in history by the blood of tens of thousands of Americans—Wilderness, Spotsylvania Court House, Yellow Tavern, Cold Harbor—the Battle of Trevilian Station became a reality due to both chance and circumstance, as is often the case in war. Located in central Virginia, the nearby carnage of previous encounters and yet-to-come engagements of the North and South could bypass this piece of ground for only so long.

The battle, fought on June 11 and 12 of 1864, was an attempt by General Grant, by way of his supreme cavalry commander, Philip Sheridan, to tear up and disrupt as much of the Confederate rail supply lines feeding the Army of Northern Virginia as possible. (This was never a very successful endeavor, as tracks were often quickly repaired.) In addition, Grant wanted to create a diversion so that he could have time to get his troops (some 100,000) across the James River and attack Petersburg before the Rebels could reinforce their fortifications. Grant also believed (perhaps rightly) that once the attack on Petersburg occurred, Lee might counterattack, and it would give his overwhelming numbers a chance to destroy Lee. Logistically speaking, it was a good plan; however, in actuality, even those plans that look so promising on paper or in the generals' discussions never seem to unfold as anticipated. History has a tendency to play out in unforeseen ways.

Sheridan set out from Cold Harbor on June 7, 1864, with two divisions of troops. By the next day, advance units of Confederate scouts got wind of his departure and sent the intel back to their superiors, who understood exactly his intentions: The Federals were attempting to destroy the railroad junctions at Charlottesville and Gordonville, and beyond, if possible. The Confederates began to make plans of their own. Once the battle commenced, it would involve four divisions of cavalry (two Union and two Confederate) consisting of approximately nine thousand Union troops to the Rebels' almost seven thousand, and it would go down in the history books as the largest cavalry battle of the Civil War.

The Southerners reached Trevilian Station before Sheridan's divisions and set up four encampments, all of them south of Gordonsville Road, stretching from just west of Trevilian Station and running east to Louisa. Both sides understood that the battle would begin the next morning, and by 6:30 a.m. Sheridan would be at the business he knew best. Placing a high degree of confidence in Custer's good judgment during a hot battle (something he'd witnessed over and over again, and wouldn't decry till Little Bighorn), he allowed him to separate from the main command. General Custer and his brigade of Wolverines (the First, Fifth, Sixth, and Seventh Michigan Cavalry) headed toward Louisa Courthouse, while generals Wesley Merritt and Thomas Devin attacked toward the center between Trevilian Station and Custer's current route. Merritt's men were the first to close with the enemy (which benefited Custer, as the Rebels were drawn to the sound of Merritt's firing), but Custer, at the head of his men, soon clashed with elements of Confederate general Wade Hampton's division, who were anticipating such a move.

Once the way was clear, Custer drove his troops west down Nunn's Creek Road and was virtually unopposed all the way to Trevilian Station, where he immediately captured an enormous array of enemy equipment, wagons, horses, and at least several hundred men. The only problem, of course, was that the entire Rebel force in the area was even then beginning the attack on Custer, and from all sides. And Sheridan, who would almost immediately recognize the escalating volley of fire from the direction of

Trevilian Station as a sign of a sharp clash occurring with his boy general, would still not reach him in time to be of any assistance. Custer's brigade was beginning to take significant fire from the enemy, causing the blue-clad troopers to begin dropping all around. Soon they were completely surrounded, and would pay dearly in their fight to escape. Writing later of the battle, Custer told Libbie, "My Brigade was completely surrounded, and attacked on all sides. Had the others been prompt we would have struck the greatest blow inflicted by our cavalry."[6] According to Custer, his lightning-speed ride to Trevilian Station was well within Sheridan's plan, and there seemed to be more than a little resentment when others failed to carry out their end of things. Custer wrote: "I was ordered to go to Trevilian Station, there to form a junction with two other brigades. I carried out instructions to the letter, but the others were three hours behind me."[7] In this respect, Custer cannot be faulted for his actions.

One of the brigades attacking Custer was commanded by his old friend and fellow West Point classmate, Major General Thomas L. Rosser. Both men had great respect for one another, and it is certain both wished for the other to survive the war. That said, Rosser's men, along with the other brigades, would tear into Custer's Michigan Brigade without mercy. Bullets were crisscrossing in every direction, and the standard-bearer, a Sergeant Mashon, was shot and mortally wounded. As he handed off the flag to Custer, who ripped it from its staff and stuffed it in his shirt, Mashon muttered, "General, they have killed me. Take the flag!"[8] Custer would be hit with two spent bullets, causing only minor swelling. Later, he was nearly killed when a sharpshooter's bullet grazed him as he was moving a mortally wounded soldier to a safer place out of the line of fire. Custer's Luck seemed to be never-ending.

Not only did Custer fail to hold on to his haul of equipment, horses, and prisoners, but he also lost his own wagon that carried most of his personal items, leaving him, as he told Libbie, with little more than his toothbrush. One humorous aspect of the capture of Custer's wagon was the loss of Libbie's letters—letters of a sexual nature that were intended for their eyes only. "I regret the loss of your letters more than all else,"

Custer wrote. "I enjoyed every word you wrote, but do not relish the idea of others amusing themselves with them, particularly as some of the expressions employed. . . . Somebody must be more careful hereafter in the use of the *double entendu* [*sic*]."

The toll to his Michiganders was very high, and the fight at Trevilian Station cost upwards of four hundred casualties. But they would extricate themselves from the battle, and despite the heavy losses, there is no sign or any written indication from Custer that perhaps a more-coordinated plan of attack might have served them better at Trevilian Station. Given the manner in which George Custer would die some twelve years later, it is impossible not to draw a correlation between the rapid charge at Trevilian Station and his final battle at Little Bighorn. The key ingredient in both charges, without a doubt, is Custer's sense of invincibility, both personally and with respect to the troops he commanded. Perhaps the constant rain of lead and iron that whizzed by him during the war as he conducted battle and the spent bullets that caused only minor bruising gave him an odd sense of destiny, instilling a mind-set that would make possible his destruction in the wilds of Montana.

It is of interest to note a possible reason for Custer's fearlessness in battle—not that any single detail could account for such a life, but it does offer a glimpse into Custer's personality. In a letter to Libbie, dated May 1, 1864, Custer speaks of his feelings about divine protection from death:

> *It may seem strange to you, dear girl, that I, a non-professing (tho not an unbeliever) Christian, should so ardently desire you to remain so. I have never prayed as others do. Yet, on the eve of every battle in which I have been engaged, I have never omitted to pray inwardly, devoutly. Never have I failed to commend myself to God's keeping, asking him to forgive my past sins, and to watch over me while in danger . . . and to receive me if I fell, while caring for those near and dear to me. After having done so all anxiety for myself, here or hereafter, is dispelled. I feel that my destiny is in the hands of the almighty. This belief, more than any other fact or reason, makes me brave and fearless as I am.*[9]

The cavalry battles of 1864 would finally give way to the final days of the Civil War. Hundreds of thousands of men had died during the past four years, and despite the tenacity of President Jefferson Davis to keep the Confederacy alive, men and material were running short. By 1865, the end of their dream was well within sight. The North was running short on patience as well, as is clearly evidenced by the draft riots of the same year. Unlike the Confederates, however, the Union had an almost endless supply of men and material, and because of this, the proverbial deck of cards was stacked against the South from the beginning. For Custer, however, his boundless energy and drive kept him at the forefront of the costliest war in American history.

The battles in the Shenandoah Valley in the fall of 1864 were the most decisive of the entire Valley Campaign. Until this time, the North could not claim they had won such an initiative or had total control of this fertile and important land literally sustaining the Confederate cause, but that was about to change. On September 19, Custer, still commanding his beloved Wolverines, decisively defeated the enemy at the third battle of Winchester, Virginia. In October, generals Custer and Merritt (at this time, Custer was the new commander of the Second Cavalry Division) embarked on a new mission in the Shenandoah Valley with the intent of stripping the land of everything useful to General Lee. Anything that couldn't be carted off or served to the troops in the field (Southern livestock was being repatriated by the stroke of a pen) was to be destroyed. Implementing a scorched-earth policy, Sheridan was determined to deny the Rebels everything, and if it meant destroying the personal property of the citizens, they were going to do it. This was in direct response to the actions of General Jubal Early and his battle-seasoned cavalrymen, who had been conducting their own raids into Union territory and were a constant threat to Washington, D.C. Enraged by this policy, Custer soon found Confederate cavalry units nipping at his heels, and his superiors instructed him to do something about it.

And so, on October 9, Custer would again clash with his good friend Thomas Rosser and the men of his Laurel Division. But it would not be a repeat of Trevilian Station. This time, Rosser's men would be routed, and the battle jokingly became known as the Woodstock Races, as the Yankees killed, chased, and captured the scattered enemy troops and equipment for miles. Custer even captured a wagonload of personal items belonging to Rosser, telling Libbie, "I attacked Genl. Rosser's Division of 3 brigades with my Division of 2, and gained the most glorious victory. I drove Rosser in confusion 10 miles, captured 6 cannon, all his advance trains, ambulance train, all Genls. [sic] Rosser's, Lomax's, & Wickham's headquarters wagons containing all their baggage, private & official papers . . . I am now arrayed in Genl. Rosser's coat."[10] Custer even recovered an ambrotype (early photograph) of his beloved Libbie that had been lost in the fighting at Trevilian Station when his wagon was captured.

On October 19, Custer smashed through and routed the forces of Jubal Early, stripping him of much of his ability to conduct war. Those who survived and were fortunate enough to escape capture were taken in by other Rebel units. The fall of 1864 was turning out to be a bloody time, but the victorious momentum was clearly with the North. On March 2, 1865, Custer would again engage and defeat Early at the battle of Waynesboro, and the beleaguered commander of the Army of the Valley would barely escape capture.

In early November 1864, Custer brought his nineteen-year-old brother Tom on board the Sixth Michigan Cavalry, granting him the rank of second lieutenant. Like his brother, Thomas Custer was devoid of fear, and was absolutely relentless when attacking the enemy. Of course, he had seen plenty of bloodletting during the war after enlisting (at the age of sixteen) in the Twenty-First Ohio Infantry in September of 1861 and participating in numerous engagements. Yet it would be here, fighting in the saddle beside his older sibling, that Tom Custer would distinguish himself by winning two Congressional Medals of Honor—the first at Namozine Church on April 3, 1865, and the second, during the fighting at Sayler's Creek three days later. On both occasions he leapt over the

Confederate line and grabbed the Rebel flag from its bearer. The first happened without a hitch—Tom even captured prisoners—however, he was nearly killed at Sayler's Creek when the color-bearer fired his pistol. The bullet grazed Tom's face and neck, causing him to momentarily reel in the saddle. Within a second, however, Tom had steadied himself and fired his revolver, killing the soldier instantly and capturing the flag. Such fearless actions in battle brought a smile to the face of George Custer.

Custer's star would continue to rise during the Appomattox Campaign in the closing days of the war. At no time, even though the end of the slaughter was plainly in sight, did he ever shrink from battle. Custer would continue the same actions against the enemy he had always employed: Attack whenever possible, defeat them soundly, and worry not about one's personal safety. This was the Custer creed, and it was well known on both sides of the lines. Custer would throw himself at the enemy at every opportunity, and his contribution to the ending of the war would not go unnoticed by generals Sheridan, Grant, and even President Lincoln himself. At places like Dinwiddie Court House, Five Forks, Sayler's Creek (where they trapped and defeated one-quarter of the retreating Rebel army), and Appomattox Station, Custer proved his worth and forever linked himself with this tumultuous time in the nation's history. Once the Confederates lost Petersburg (it took years for the Union to take it), and Richmond had to be evacuated, General Lee's only hope was to flee with his army and regroup at a later date. But the Yankee cavalry, with Custer always at the forefront, was hemming him in on all sides. It was a bleak situation for a cause that was now in its final death struggle.

An interesting aside: Only hours prior to generals Robert E. Lee and Ulysses S. Grant signing the documents of surrender at the McLean house on April 9, 1865, Custer and Confederate general James Longstreet had an encounter that did not turn out as Custer had imagined it would. Having ridden into Longstreet's camp "at a fast gallop" by way of a Confederate escort, Custer demanded the immediate and unconditional surrender of the Rebel army. Longstreet, being direct without being insulting, stopped him cold and reminded him "that I was not the commander of the army, and that he was within the lines of the enemy without authority, addressing a superior officer, and in disrespect to General Grant and as well as myself; that if I was the commander of the army I would not receive the message of general Sheridan." At this, Custer became more compliant, so Longstreet told him that Lee and Grant were even then meeting "to determine the future of the armies."[11] Custer then returned to his side of the line.

Grant and Lee did meet later that afternoon to sign the formal papers of surrender, and Custer was on the grounds of the McLean house as the historic occasion was unfolding. Indeed, he spent the time gabbing with now-former enemies, and for the boy general, there wasn't even the slightest bit of animosity for those who had defended the Southern cause. They were friends again, and the Union had been preserved. General Philip Sheridan was so pleased with Custer's contribution to the conflict that he purchased the table upon which the formal papers of surrender were signed and gave it to Custer as a gift for his wife. A letter from Sheridan to Libbie expresses just what her husband meant to him: "My dear Madam—I respectfully present to you the small writing-table on which the conditions for the surrender of the Confederate Army of Northern Virginia were written by Lt. General Grant—and permit me to say, Madam, that there is scarcely an individual in our service who has contributed more to bring this about than your very gallant husband."[12]

The costliest and the bloodiest war fought on the North American continent was now over, and George Armstrong Custer had come through it virtually intact. He had done more than his fair share during the war, and had gained a name for himself that he couldn't have imagined on the day he left West Point and headed for Washington at the start of the war. He was loved and had the thanks of a grateful nation; he had married a woman he adored and would be with for the rest of his life; and he had (at least for a time) satiated his inner need to kill and expose himself to the lethal atmosphere of war, where at any moment he could be obliterated or horribly maimed or disabled. None of that mattered. The *possible* results just didn't enter into the equation for Custer. He believed that the ongoing tornado of destruction and heartache for those involved was a reasonable price to pay in order to be able to fellowship with the dark impulses of that mistress. So far, he'd been able to indulge himself with her at little to no cost. And this "luck" he had experienced through-out the years of the war would continue well into the future.

But if the dead of war could speak, every soldier that has fallen in battle would tell you it only takes one bad moment, on one very unfor-tunate day, and the unthinkable will occur and take from you everything you've ever known. That day for Custer was now eleven years, two months, and sixteen days in the future.

As a warrior, Custer's best years were now behind him. The glorious victories he had achieved fighting the Confederates, and the stature he had attained in the war to preserve the Union, would never be found in his postwar duty in the Southern states. Of course, there were "enemies" to the west, in territories inhabited by nomadic tribes of Native Ameri-cans (a term unheard of then). The time would come when the pow-ers that be would need an orderly westward expansion, and the ultimate clash of cultures would, over time, demand a permanent solution. As this drama unfolded, George Armstrong Custer would be annihilated, and that annihilation would reverberate through time. Sadly, his achievements during the Civil War would be forgotten by all but a relative few students of that period of American history. His new fame, or infamy, would have its beginning and ending in one of the worst military defeats of all time. Ironically, the word *defeat*, up until that moment, had never had a place in George Custer's vocabulary.

One could say that the final, official act of the war between the North and South was the parade held in Washington, D.C., on May 23 and 24, 1865. It was to honor those who had sacrificed so much to preserve the Union. Of course, there were hundreds of thousands of dead who couldn't attend, and many thousands of wounded too severely disabled to march in the great blue throng (or even stand on the sidelines), but it must have been a grand sight to see for those attending. Philip Sheridan, dispatched by Grant to Louisiana (Custer would soon be joining him), could not attend, and so while General Wesley Merritt led the parade of cavalry, General Custer rode proudly at the head of his Third Cavalry Division. Looking resplendent in his crisp uniform, he rode Don Juan (a beloved mount), but due to an overzealous bystander who apparently tossed some type of wreath at Custer, the horse bolted and ran like the wind past the grandstand. Because of this unscheduled display of equine prowess, Custer had to trot back and retrieve his dropped sword and broad-brimmed hat that had blown from his head.

When the cavalry had cleared the parade, they made their way back to their nearby campgrounds just outside the city. A stirring of emotions filled Custer and all involved, for the end of their wartime association had come, and even though they all welcomed peace, it was still a truly bittersweet moment. Writing of it years later, Libbie said: "Down the line rode their yellow-haired 'boy-general,' waving his hat, but setting his teeth and trying to hold with iron nerve the quivering muscles of his speaking face; keeping his eyes wide open, that the moisture dimming their vision might not gather and fall."[13]

CHAPTER 4

West Is His Destiny

At the close of the Civil War, Custer's place in history had been firmly established. Or so it seemed. At the age of twenty-four he had attained greatness as a fearless military icon whose decisions in battle had the respect of friend and foe alike. As a renowned war hero, his prospects seemed numerous. But postwar fame would be harder to come by, and anything less than actual combat would leave George Custer feeling unfulfilled. Happily, he was completely fulfilled as a husband, and whatever the future held for Autie and Libbie, they were determined to experience it together.

Their journey began in May of 1865, when the couple took a steamboat down the Mississippi River to New Orleans, where Custer was to report to Major General Sheridan. Sheridan had orders from General Grant to crush any Rebel factions still operating in the area, and to keep an eye open for developing changes in Mexico where a national upheaval was occurring. To be sure, General Sheridan was pleased to have generals Custer and Merritt back, for they were commanders he could depend on to do his bidding. Custer had no idea as they stepped off the boat into New Orleans, a bastion of Southern hospitality, that he was entering a world heretofore unknown to him as a commander of men. The days of love and admiration were now over. He would be engaging in another dimension of soldiering, where his personality—forged in war—would clash not only with those under his command, but fellow officers as well. Throughout these coming years, and to a great extent, because of them, Custer would be forced to rely on the powerful reinforcement of his wife and his inner circle of very close officers and family members.

An interesting aside regarding the couple's trip south was Custer's ongoing, good-natured, and magnanimous attitude regarding his former enemies. During this trip, which began in Louisville, Kentucky, Custer got wind that a former enemy, General John Bell Hood, had joined the boat for a while. Custer wasted no time in locating him and engaging him in conversation. Hood, who had left a leg on the field of battle, was using crutches, and when Libbie joined the men at Custer's request, the general had a bit of trouble rising from his chair. Libbie described him as "tall, fair, dignified, and soldierly." Hood, apparently as jovial and happy as Custer was to be conversing about the war, had been severely wounded twice during the conflict. The first injury occurred on July 2, 1863, during the second day of fighting at Gettysburg, where he lost the use of his left arm. The leg was left on the battlefield of Chickamauga just two months later. Keeping a strong sense of humor, Hood told Libbie that of the five different "artificial" legs he had tried, "English, German, French, Yankee, and Confederate—the Yankee was the best of all."[1] As Hood was departing the boat, Libbie noted that Custer helped "the maimed hero [and] we bade him goodbye with real regret."[2] It was clear to Libbie that such meetings between former enemies meant quite a lot to both parties, for the two shared a common bond only warriors can know, and each understood exactly where the other was coming from.

The city of New Orleans held a great deal of fascination for the Custers. Visiting the French Quarter, dinning at myriad fine restaurants, where, as Libbie related, "we saw eating made a fine art,"[3] and walking among the shops and people allowed the happy couple to enjoy themselves as carefree tourists. While in the city, Custer also developed a love for Southern coffee, and forever after compared even the best Northern blend as being "almost equal to the French Market."[4] But duty called, and any semblance of a normal civilian existence was but a mirage, for while the delicacies of even the good life may have satisfied for a day or two, it couldn't compare to the thrill of the open territory and the possibility of battle. The Custers, on orders from General Sheridan, would soon board a steamer for the trip to Alexandria, Louisiana, and the unknown future that awaited them.

On the horizon the proverbial pot was already boiling with the possibility of a war in Mexico, and indeed, the likelihood of full-scale conflict
existed there. Just two years earlier the French had installed their own man,
Ferdinand Maximilian, as emperor of the country, driving out Mexico's
legitimate leader, Benito Juarez. As such, the United States was considering its option of an "invasion" of Mexico, should the president deem it
necessary. But even this wasn't the only threat of violence: As a "conquering" army, it fell to Custer, Merritt, and all uniforms blue to see that law
and order were maintained, which would present problems and surprises
of its own. Indeed, there were plenty of Confederate veterans in the area
who were angry about losing the war. They were upset about the economic
upheaval and the general ruin of the South, and had difficulty swallowing
their pride every time they encountered a blue uniform. It must also be
said that these former Rebels had legitimate gripes with some of the Yankees who were wandering around their part of the world and, whenever it
suited them, stealing from the citizenry. There was little the locals could
do about it, and Sheridan, who wasn't about to condone such actions, told
Custer to see to it that they were brought to an abrupt halt.

Once in Alexandria, Custer assembled a fighting force from a combination of volunteer Midwestern cavalry units. It is important here to
point out the differences between Custer and the men under him at this
time as compared to the relationship Custer had with his troopers during the Civil War. First, the men who served under Custer during this
venture in the Southwest were cavalrymen who'd fought the war bravely
in the Western theater, just as Custer's men had, but now that it was
over, they very much wanted to return to their homes. They were, in fact,
citizen soldiers who had come together during the war when they realized their country needed them. They knew nothing of West Point or
soldiering in peacetime, and they had no desire to play policemen in a
former Confederate state now that the war was over. They were saddle-
sore, tired, and thankful they hadn't been killed in the cataclysmic events
of 1861–65, and they were in no mood to be killed now. Once Custer
became aware of these issues, he felt no sympathy at all for the men, and

in fact considered them insubordinate whenever their complaints were laid before him. Their attitude, Custer believed, was anything but soldier-like, and he could not let such actions go without being confronted. In Custer's mind, the idea that anyone would ever desire to return home to a peacetime environment when the exciting life of being a soldier was available was unthinkable. This mind-set was foreign to Custer and his Civil War band of brothers. The new breed of trooper turned out to be very frustrating for Custer, and his dislike for them was revealed in his actions—or, should we say, his lack of action.

One bright spot in all of this for Custer was that he did (or soon would) have his family with him, which made the lack of cohesion he'd experience with his troops a bit more bearable. Besides Libbie, Emanuel Custer had been hired as a forager. Brother Tom, who had fought along-side Custer during the war, was now a permanent fixture at his side and would follow wherever he would lead. In fact, in the coming years, Custer would lean heavily on this inner circle for moral support. Not everyone would be allowed to enter this close-quarter realm of the general's, which in turn, would produce an arrogant "us versus them" mentality.

The Custers arrived in Alexandria in late June of that year, and took up residence in an abandoned plantation house. Immediately upon arrival, Custer began forming the five volunteer cavalry regiments into two bri-gades. It was hot and humid, and mosquitoes would prove to be an ever-present enemy to this already-dispirited group. They would not be staying in Alexandria for very long. By August, the soldiers would endure an arduous march to Hempstead, Texas, some 240 miles away.

One event prior to this march exemplifies the egregious way Custer treated his men once his authority had been challenged. Under Custer's stern hand were the following regiments: First Iowa, Second Wiscon-sin, Twelfth and Fifteenth Illinois, and the Seventh Indiana, comprising some 4,500 veterans of the Civil War. During the weeks prior to the trip to Hempstead, a number of commissioned and noncommissioned offi-cers of the Second Wisconsin presented a petition that would force the resignation of their leader, Lieutenant Colonel N. H. Dale. Custer very wisely met this challenge to his authority by arresting the commissioned officers and reducing in rank the noncommissioned. Although the petitioners genuinely wanted Dale removed, they weren't about to suffer such an extreme penalty, and soon all the men withdrew their names from the petition—all, that is, except one.[5] The lone voice now calling for Dale's expulsion was Sergeant Leonard Lancaster, considered to be a good and faithful soldier, well liked throughout the regiment. Of course, attempting to force a superior officer to resign can be considered mutinous, and can lead to a court-martial. Because Lancaster refused to remove his name from the petition, he was quickly found guilty and sentenced to execution by firing squad. Without question, Lancaster was both a brave and principled man, but his stance was leading him to a pine box if some intervention didn't occur. That help began when Dale, the object of the current problem, drew up a petition for Lancaster to be pardoned. This was signed not only by all commissioned officers of the Second Wisconsin, but by Custer's officers as well.[6]

But no pardon was forthcoming from Custer, although it is almost certain he wasn't about to have Lancaster shot, as even Lancaster expected by this time. When some suggested they were willing to free him, Lancaster responded by saying, "I'll stay here; I am guilty of no crime and I would die a hundred deaths rather than play the part of a coward, and I'll never be called a deserter. I shall be shot tomorrow night. Let them shoot me if they want to. I shall die with clean hands and a clean conscience."[7]

Custer, fully aware of Lancaster's intransigence, decided to let theatrics rule the day. Instead of saving the sergeant prior to the day of execution—even though Custer had already been made aware of death threats against him—he lined the troops up to witness Lancaster's and another man's (a deserter) execution. With rifles aimed at the two soon-to-be-departed and the executioners aligning their sighting eye with their targets, Custer allowed the commands of *Ready* and then *Aim* before he had Lancaster removed from the line of fire. The last command of *Fire* was given, and in one combined volley, the deserter was immediately killed.

Pulling Lancaster out of the line at the last moment had little positive effect. Most of the men despised Custer, and that sentiment would not change. Indeed, their hatred for their commander would only increase in the days ahead as the cavalrymen headed to Hempstead, for it was during this march (as well as their time at Hempstead) that the authoritarian rule of the boy general would be most evident. It was an arduous journey of some 240 miles, and the command would make it in nineteen days. Hot, tired, and ill equipped with respect to rations, the troopers were forbidden to forage for food (or anything else the barren countryside might contain) on their own, and in fact, could not leave their places in the column. Any infraction of Custer's edicts resulted in a lashing of biblical proportions (twenty-five lashes seemed to be the standard) and the shaving of the head. Of course, Custer had already demonstrated his willingness to use the firing squad in answer to desertions, so soldiers knew they would abandon their duties at their own peril. Even this wouldn't matter, for the conditions would prove to be so deplorable that even the threat of death could not deter some of the troops from deserting. Of course, their rumbling stomachs spoke louder than the dictatorial outbursts of their commander, and when some of the men were caught stealing livestock to obtain a decent meal, the flogging and the shaving began. The conditions during the march, as well as during their time in Hempstead, can aptly be described as horrific: intense heat and humidity, legions of insects, lack of proper food and medical care, and a commander who was out of touch with his men. It was a cauldron of problems that could have boiled over into a genuine mutiny and the killing of Custer, but as was always the case when danger approached, Custer never flinched, and somehow, he survived the crisis.

Life for Custer and his wife, brother, and father was not unpleasant at all. The difficulties experienced by the rank and file were not a part of their world, and Custer would combat the boredom of a peaceful military life with hunting, playing pranks on his father, and enjoying life with Libbie. As always, the Custers hobnobbed with the well-heeled (or formerly well-heeled) of the area. Even so, the extreme tedium of peace was not an element in which Custer could excel; he certainly didn't enjoy it, and it stood in stark contrast to the environment of the Civil War. Not only was Custer up to the task of whatever the war threw at him, but it provided the ideal realm in which his capabilities could be revealed. This is why the men who served under the boy general during those tumultuous years gave him their full allegiance. Custer led by example, and the respect he earned by his actions produced the strong bond forged in war. Here in the Lone Star State, none of that existed. To the men who served under him in Louisiana and Texas, he was an ogre, and nothing more.

By October of that year, the command had left Hempstead and marched 124 miles to Austin, their new base of operation. By November, the Second Wisconsin was mustered out to the great relief of its troops. Soon others would follow, and by February of 1866, Custer would be reduced in rank from brevet major general of US Volunteers (a rank bestowed on him after Appomattox), to captain in the Fifth United States Cavalry. His not-so-beloved force of disgruntled volunteers was finally allowed to return to their homes, and the Custers would make their way back to Monroe, Michigan.[8] Sheridan had earlier attempted to convince Custer to apply for the rank of brevet major general in the regular army, but he either dawdled in his actions or had no intention of acting on Sheridan's advice. For now, however, he would be at the pay grade of captain. The future was starting to look like one big question mark to Custer, and he was determined to find a successful endeavor to throw himself into.

There would be thoughts, however brief, of making his mark in either the railroad or mining industries, or even politics. As there wasn't a well-informed person within the country who hadn't heard of the young war hero, he was welcomed at the tables of the rich and influential in New York after making his way there to test the waters. Surrounded by both money and power, the young warrior quickly felt sparked by another kind of excitement. Wherever he was recognized, he was hailed for his wartime exploits, and accolades filled the air. It must have all been quite heady for the twenty-seven-year-old, but he'd earned it on those bloody and hellish battlefields, and now it was much like food for the soul. Custer savored every minute of it. In a letter to Libbie (she had stayed behind in Monroe), Custer sums up his feelings about life there: "Oh, these New York people are so kind to me. I would like to become wealthy in order to make my permanent home here."[9] But neither these new careers nor politics would pan out for Custer; it just wasn't in his makeup to even enter that world. Custer was a soldier, and he would never be fulfilled in any other occupation. Though he longed to be wealthy to give Libbie the kind of life he believed she both wanted and deserved, such dreams, if they were to occur at all, would have to be realized through his life as a soldier and his connection to war. If any civilian occupation were ever going to be a part of his life, it wouldn't be for the foreseeable future, and Custer understood this.

War in Mexico never materialized on his watch, and it wouldn't be long before the French would abandon the country. The toppling of their puppet, Emperor Maximilian, would eventually take place. This might have produced a moment of sadness for Custer (although joyfully welcomed by the troops), as it meant there would be no battle between two worthy armies, and no sustained bloodletting. But all was not lost. Early 1866 also brought the offer from Mexico for Custer to join the army of Benito Juarez as adjutant general, with a whopping salary of $16,000 a year (well over $200,000 today). It would call for a leave of absence for up to a year, Custer reasoned. Loving war as he did, and contemplating such a financial windfall to do that which he loved, he asked for and received permission to head south of the border from General Grant and Secretary of War Edwin Stanton, but the move was blocked by Secretary of State William H. Seward, who believed the French government wouldn't like it.[10] The only way Custer could fulfill his desire to fight in Mexico was to resign his position in the army, and there wasn't any way he was going to do that. Had Custer been able to become adjutant general in the army of Juarez, replicating there the kind of victories he had attained during the war, it might have seemed like little more than an extension of his duties as an officer of Uncle Sam. Thwarted, his hunger for the sights and sounds of full-scale warfare would have to wait. He would hear again the sharp cracks of rifles and pistols being unleashed at an enemy, but it would not be in a war under the Mexican flag. His desire to be in the saddle leading men in the midst of life-and-death conflict would again be offered to him, but for now, patience would have to rule the day.

One incident worth mentioning from Custer's time in the Southwest was his inability to control his emotions when dealing with insubordinate officers. This is the first of two such events (the second will involve a very public dispute with Captain Frederick Benteen), either of which could have easily resulted in his death or an embarrassing court-martial. In both instances, Custer responded in an unmilitary fashion, based, I believe, on his inflated image of himself, along with his juvenile schoolboy tactics which always seemed to be very close to the surface of his personality.

In this first incident, Custer became angry when he learned that a disgruntled captain with the First Iowa had written home about the hellish march from Alexandria to Hempstead, and someone on the receiving end had submitted the letter for publication in the local newspaper. The captain, of course, laid all of their troubles on Custer, and when confronted by him, the man refused to retract it. Custer immediately flew into a rage and grabbed a "horsewhip,"[11] with the clear intention of physically attacking the offender. Not wishing to submit to a beating, the captain was in the process of drawing his sword from its sheath when Major Jacob Greene walked in and quickly put a stop to it. Custer's rash decision was little more than an invitation to a backyard brawl, yet the end result would have been far worse. One would think that in retrospect, Custer would have come to see the wisdom of not behaving in this manner, but years later, almost the exact same scenario would occur, and the end result would prove to be an embarrassment to the leader of the Seventh Cavalry.

—◆—

Custer's directionless season would end in the spring of 1866, when he was commissioned a lieutenant colonel in the newly formed Seventh Cavalry. He could not at this time fathom what this westward move would mean to him or the love he would develop for life on the Great Plains.

Neither could he grasp what warfare would be like in this world of big sky, open ranges, plentiful game, strange weather, and the peculiar habits of the current, albeit nomadic residents. He would never doubt his mission, or the ability of the United States to accomplish its goal in dealing with the problems associated with westward expansion. While sympathizing with the plight of the Native Americans, his contribution was to carry out orders and leave the politicking to others. This mind-set, along with his never-ending thirst for conflict, meant that Custer and his Seventh Cavalry were destined to play a prominent role in whatever changes were to come. They would be in the thick of it, and in this respect, it would mirror his time during the Civil War. But here the likeness would end, for war with the Indians would be nothing like war with the South. This would be a war of cultures, and the deep-seated hatred that existed between the combatants would intensify and culminate in the shattering of one culture and the unexpected death of an iconic leader of the other. It was, above all things, a portrait of abuse and greed, producing lasting results which can be witnessed today.

Fort Riley was established as a military outpost in 1853, in answer to the opening of the Santa Fe and Oregon Trails, which started receiving travelers in the 1830s. This fort was like all the others established throughout the Kansas frontier—Wallace, Larned, Leavenworth, Scott, Hays, Harker, and Dodge—in that it would have elements of both cavalry and infantry, with perhaps no more than two hundred troops per fort. These forts owed their very existence to the flood of white settlers, trappers, hunters, and a host of people who believed a better life would be found in these wide-open spaces. The allure of the West meant this flow would not just continue but would eventually explode. Not surprisingly, this great human trek placed an enormous burden on the Indians, and the army, acting as a reactionary police force, was responsible for handling the problem. But nothing is ever as simple as it seems. Their mission was also to keep a close eye on those Indian tribes living within Kansas as they were settled on their respective reservations, and ensuring that interactions between Indian tribes, and, indeed, between the entire

Indian population and the whites, went smoothly and were violence-free. These Indians were, for the most part, the conquered tribes, but conquered didn't mean dead, and often the young braves of these subjugated Indians would look for ways to get back at the "invaders," and it fell to the army to exact retribution.

Yet this wasn't the military's only concern, as the Great Plains were filled with tribes such as the Sioux and Cheyenne who were not compliant and didn't feel that they needed to be. After all, they reasoned, who were these white people to tell them what to do? It was a strong argument that even many whites could identify with. The Indians must have been exceedingly sorry to see the bloody war between the whites end. Now that hostilities had eased, westward expansion would begin anew.

By September of 1866 the Custers had arrived at Fort Riley, located in northeast Kansas. Having taken the Union Pacific Railroad to the end of the line, the Custers still had another ten miles to travel by wagon until the fort, sitting on a plateau, finally came into view. Traveling with them was Eliza, Custer's invaluable cook, who was always in the "thick of it," especially at Trevilian Station. Here, the Seventh Cavalry, consisting of twelve companies, began assembling for frontier duty. Of course, it was rare to have more than two or three companies of cavalry and/or infantry at any one fort at a given time, but the troops would come together for expeditions.[12] Life on the Western frontier could be drudgery for the common soldier, and it wasn't much better for the officers overseeing them. Many would seek solace in a bottle. Indeed, the problem with alcohol was far greater with those serving in these rather remote outposts than those engaged in regular army duty back east, and Custer, who did all the drinking he was ever going to do back in Monroe, was quite vocal with newcomers concerning the regiment's need for sobriety.

The Custers did not share the depression felt by some who were learning to cope with life on the frontier. On the contrary, they found the expanse of their surroundings breathtaking. Nothing back east could compare with life out here, and for many who ventured this way, it produced a euphoria that could not be equaled anywhere else. Custer was, above all things, a man who required a life that always challenged him. Here in the West, that desire to launch out into the unknown, to attack and conquer all obstacles in his path, was ever present, and the opportunities for glory were endless.

The commander of the Seventh Cavalry was a crusty old officer by the name of Andrew J. Smith. Colonel Smith, who had graduated from West Point during the same year George Custer was conceived, had many years of fighting Indians under his belt, and had also commanded troops in the Western theater during the Civil War. However, the actual command of the regiment would fall to Custer, for on February 27, Smith took command of the District of the Upper Arkansas. It is not known whether Custer ever sought the wisdom of Smith concerning the perils of Indian fighting, but it would have been a wise thing for him to do. Smith understood the Indians' capabilities, and Custer would have benefited from such knowledge.

Like many forts in the Western theater, Fort Riley did not have connecting walls between structures, but was designed with an open expanse that was bordered by the various buildings. Libbie found this to be especially challenging, as the whipping gusts of wind could lift a lady's dress above her head without a moment's notice. "As the post was on a plateau, the wind from the two river valleys swept over it constantly. The flag was torn to ribbons in no time. . . ." She and Autie quickly thwarted nature: "He thought out a plan," Libbie recalled, "which he helped me carry into effect, by cutting bits of lead in small strips, and these I sewed into the hem. Thus loaded down, we took our constitutional about the post, and outwitted the elements. . . ."[13] Wind or no wind, the fields around Fort Riley were well traversed by the Custers on horseback, and they found great joy riding together. On one occasion while galloping side by side, Custer reached over and lifted Libbie from her saddle. These were heady times for the Custers. There wasn't yet a hint of danger as their mounts tore into the Kansas prairie and the fort took shape under the general's leadership.

Tom would soon join them at Fort Riley. The brothers would be together again for a new adventure, with a new enemy, and there wasn't the slightest reason to suspect anything would be different this time around. Hidden from them, however, was the fact that their own personal hourglass was already draining away, and that its last grain of sand would fall in less than ten years.

It's not as if Custer was itching for an Indian War—at least, not publicly at this time, and certainly not in print. He made clear the disadvantages of such a thing in his writings for *Galaxy* magazine, articles which were penned from Fort Riley and would later receive an even wider audience after being published as *My Life on the Plains*. Quoting an editorial from one of the New York papers, Custer wrote, "There are two classes of people who are always eager to get up an Indian war—the army and our frontiersmen." Custer then set the record straight as he saw it: "That this statement was honestly made I do not doubt, but that instead of being true it could not have been farther from the truth . . . I assert . . . that of all classes of our population, the army and the people living on the frontier entertain the greatest dread of an Indian war, and are willing to make the greatest sacrifices to avoid its horrors."[14]

Horrors or not, an Indian war was coming.

By the spring of 1867, the clash of these two cultures was taking a drastic turn, and this period would mark the beginning of Custer and his Seventh Cavalry's march toward destiny. The white expansion had inflamed the hearts and minds of the native people, and, still possessing the ability to resist, they were going to do so. Those in Washington knew what was coming, and despite the resistance on moral grounds from those fellow citizens who understood the problems inherent with westward expansion, and the subsequent raw deal the Indians were receiving, the current leadership would have it no other way. As one historian so correctly noted, "Whites had steadily encroached upon Indian lands, and new treaties of cessation had been negotiated from time to time to validate the incursions."[15] Whenever anyone would speak out concerning the ill treatment of the Indian, such attempts "ultimately foundered on the deep-seated conviction that the white man had a superior right to the land."[16] And if the past was any indication of future bloodletting, things were going to become horrendous indeed. Indeed, two events, one in 1864 and the other in 1866, were without question forerunners to the clash at Little Bighorn, the apex of the war in the West.

Only a couple of years earlier, the bloodthirsty events of what became known as the Sand Creek Massacre telegraphed in no uncertain terms the true intention of the whites when it came to warfare with the Indians. What would happen here would not be forgotten by the Sioux, the Cheyenne, and all the other tribes of the Great Plains who valued their own version of freedom. It was a line of demarcation in the affairs between whites and Indians, and neither side would soon forget what happened there.

On November 28, 1864, Colonel John M. Chivington, forty-three, led nearly eight hundred men of his First and Third Colorado Regiments, along with some additional troops of New Mexico volunteers, to the outskirts of Chief Black Kettle's Southern Cheyenne, encamped along Sand Creek in Colorado. Having marched out of Fort Lyon some forty miles away, Chivington knew Black Kettle and his band of Cheyenne were not at war with the United States, as he had led his people to the fort just a short time earlier and proclaimed his peaceful intentions. Flying above his camp was an American flag. The "troops" who would do the killing were, for the most part, one-hundred-day volunteers, and they lacked the discipline of the regular army. Their leader, the portly Chivington, was driven by abject hatred for the Indians, and he would garner an infamous place in history because of the attack.

Chivington, a former minister, had tossed aside his Bible to kill Confederates during the Civil War. No doubt believing that alcohol would serve as an enhancer to men bent on violence, he allowed his volunteers to drink heavily prior to the Sand Creek Massacre. Before attacking Black Kettle's village, he gave this instruction: "Kill and scalp all big and little. Nits make lice."[17] In complete obedience to the "Fighting Parson," as he was called, his troops responded with a zest and determination that would make any bloodthirsty ghoul proud. Without hesitation, little children were killed while begging for their lives; some were shot, while others had their heads bashed in with the butts of rifles. All of this was done with the approval of the colonel, although later on, Chivington would disavow having any knowledge that such atrocities ever occurred. How one evolves from minister to child-killer is beyond comprehension, but he did, and before the firing stopped, over two hundred Cheyenne were dead, two-thirds of them women and children. The elderly, unable to run away or mount an adequate defense, were killed as well. Amid the terrible carnage, Black Kettle barely escaped with his life. Unbeknownst to the Cheyenne chief, his days were numbered, for the nightmarish events of Sand Creek would be visited upon him again in little more than four years, when Custer would come calling in much the same way. This time, however, there would be no escape.

It is unlikely that Custer gave it much thought when he heard of the 1864 slaughter of Black Kettle's camp. Certainly, the cost to white forces was minimal, with just fifteen soldiers killed and a small number wounded. Yet one event that happened in late December 1866 (when Custer was just getting settled at Fort Riley) may have sent a chill up his back. I mention it here because of the similarities between this incident—and the individual responsible for it—and Custer's mistakes at the Battle of Little Bighorn a decade later. It should have acted as a warning to Custer, a sober reminder of what can occur if things go wrong, no matter who the enemy might be. But this truth bounced off Custer like bullets ricocheting off of a stone wall, and did not produce the necessary caution that could have aided him in his decision-making at Little Bighorn. Most likely, the following story was considered by him to be little more than a collection of unhappy facts about an unlucky fellow officer, whose fate will be remembered and deposited in that metaphorical book of military disasters. Little did Custer realize that one day his own name would be added to this inglorious list, and that his beloved Seventh Cavalry would have a prominent chapter of its own.

On December 21, 1866, William J. Fetterman, accompanied by a force of eighty men, rushed out of Fort Phil Kearny to aid in the deliverance of the wood train that was once again under attack by the Indians. Fort Phil Kearny, located near the present-day town of Sheridan, Wyoming, was a constant hotbed of activity, and the Indians had become very adept at killing the blue-coated soldiers who were stationed there. December 21 would prove to be an especially good day for these persistent warriors.

The commanding officer of the fort, Colonel Henry B. Carrington, was forty-three years old and displayed the type of caution one might expect to find in a man of middle age. Carrington also recognized the rash nature which boiled within the heart of the young captain. Like Custer, Fetterman enjoyed battle and had seen plenty of action fighting the Confederates. Also like Custer, he felt that the US military would always be able to whip the Indians, no matter how large their numbers. The most striking common denominator would be that both men would be swallowed up in a deadly abyss of enraged Indians, and both would be remembered primarily for their deaths, and the slaughter of their men.

Before Fetterman's troops dashed out of the safety of the fort, Carrington's orders were clear. He was not to attack the Indians, but was to support the wood train only. Carrington specified: "Under no circumstances pursue over the ridge, that is, Lodge Trail Ridge."[18] Carrington must have sensed that Fetterman would disobey, as he sent a Lieutenant Wands to repeat the order before the doomed command was out of the gate. Yet within a short time, Captain Fetterman would cross Lodge Trail Ridge, and Carrington would be powerless to stop him.

Acting as decoys, a small party of warriors was successful in coaxing Fetterman into chasing them to a spot just over Lodge Trail Ridge, where they would all be overwhelmed and killed. If one stands today on this still-rural spot of land, it is easy to see why the Indians chose it, and why Carrington was so adamant that Fetterman not cross it. But Captain Fetterman suffered from that notorious disease of the mind that caused him to believe his decisions were always sound, and that the Indians were always inferior to the fighting abilities of the US Army, and as such, could never pose a true threat to a regiment of civilized soldiers.

One of the young warriors that played a prominent role in the day's fighting was an Oglala Sioux by the name of Crazy Horse, who, ten years later, would play another important role during the battle at Little Big-horn. He, too, would not survive the killing in this clash of cultures. Like Custer, this warrior still had many years of fighting ahead of him in 1866. His eventual death would be particularly ironic, as he would not fall on the battlefield.

From the moment the troops beheld the encirclement, the seriousness of the situation was very clear. As the battle commenced, the blue-coated soldiers (Fetterman's troops consisted of both cavalry and infantry) watched as the winter sky filled with arrows arcing through the cold Wyoming air. Backs, necks, stomachs, legs, arms, and wherever else a body can be struck, were pierced, and the ground around them soon thickened with arrows. From the moment the warriors attacked, the momentum was with them as they came after the soldiers from three sides. Unfortunately for Fetterman, the infantry, which made up two-thirds of his command, were armed with single-shot muskets. Once fired, it could take a soldier up to one minute—and under duress, longer—to reload and fire again. This would not bode well for them today. The cavalry, some twenty-seven men, did have Spencer repeating rifles, but even these were far too few in number. Add to this the shock and fear from being overwhelmed so quickly, and in less than an hour, not a single soldier was left alive. Two civilians with the doomed command, James Wheatley and Isaac Fisher, were able to kill many Indians using their sixteen-shot Henry rifles. It was reported that many pools of blood were seen dotting the ground for some distance around them.

All the soldiers were mutilated, except for bugler Adolf Metzger, who was found with a buffalo hide lying across him. He bore no marks beyond those the Indians inflicted to kill him, and he apparently went down swinging, as his dented bugle was found either within his hand or close to his body. This so impressed his attackers that they chose to honor him by covering him with the robe.

From behind the walls of the fort firing could be heard, and Carrington, no doubt juggling the twin emotions of anger and fear, immediately dispatched a company of troops to rescue Fetterman, but as they reached the top of the hill they saw the victorious Indians walking among the bodies and mutilating them. When the Indians saw the soldiers at the top of the rise, they began mocking them and motioning for them to come down the hill. Luckily for this small band of troops, the warriors did not attack, and they made their way back to Fort Phil Kearny. Carrington believed the Indians might even launch an attack on the fort now that the strength of the post had been greatly reduced, but Red Cloud thought better of it. So ended what became known as the Fetterman Massacre. Only the Custer debacle a decade later would shock the nation more.

As soon as was possible, Carrington dispatched a rider to Fort Laramie with a telegram to be sent to General Crook. The message contained an explanation of the disaster that had befallen Fetterman and asked for reinforcements, and also stated that he intended to hold the fort at all costs. Carrington ended his message with the emotional statement: "The Indians desperate, and they spare none."[19]

Such was the nature of war in the West.

CHAPTER 5

When Worlds Collide

From the moment the first white European set foot on the land which later would be called the United States of America, the fate of the American Indian was sealed. To be sure, hundreds of years would pass before the final curtain would fall at a place called Wounded Knee in the winter of 1890, but it would surely come, for the wheels of European thinking always turned in the direction of progress. The progress that was coming would mean change such as the land had never experienced. The Indians, whose strange nomadic ways were regarded by the whites as something out of the Stone Age, were an obstacle that could be tolerated for only so long. Yet it would prove to be a long struggle, filled with broken hearts and broken promises, where lives were shattered or enriched, depending on the color of one's skin. The newer, stronger culture proved through experience that what could not be had through the lying of the tongue could, and would, be obtained through the impact of a bullet. It would be harsh and unrelenting, and there would be no salvation for those outside the fold.

For Custer, it was all about being a soldier. He had always felt sympathy for the Indians, and in fact had authored a paper at West Point detailing his thoughts. He readily identified with the young warriors who did not want to conform to white rule. He, too, had a problem with authority, so the empathy between the cavalryman and Indian warrior was already firmly established within his mind. In a letter to Libbie during the summer campaign of 1867, Custer conveyed how important it was to avoid an all-out Indian war, stating what he believed were the reasons for the current problems of Indian raids in the area: "I regard the recent outrages as the work of small groups of irresponsible young men, eager for war."[1] But as a soldier in a country that was expanding at an almost unthinkable rate, forever changing the landscape, it was his duty to carry out his orders to the letter. And if the Indians were going to resist this change, those above Custer had made it very clear that the destruction of all Indians considered hostile (those who refused the "life" being offered them on the reservation) was the perfect way to handle the problem. Of course, there were many brave Indians throughout the Great Plains who were not so willing to go without a fight. No, there would be blood—lots of it—spilling on both sides, and the Indians would do everything possible to hang on to their way of life.

The summer campaign would be Custer's first taste of Indian warfare. The expedition, which began on March 26, 1867, was actually the military answer to the Fetterman slaughter which had happened only three months before. The whites were going to flex their muscles, and the Indians had every intention of flexing back. After all, in their view, white intentions had been aptly displayed at Sand Creek. So the Sioux, Cheyenne, and Arapaho were under no illusions as to the desire of their enemy to subjugate them. And subjugation is exactly what the military had in mind. General William Sherman, in charge of the Military Division of the Missouri, was anything but subtle when it came to his plans for retribution: "We must act with vindictive earnestness against the Sioux, even to their extermination, men, women, and children."[2]

Sherman may have been speaking out of rage for the killing of Fetterman and the troops, but that may be a stretch. More likely, he meant exactly what he said, and found the benefits of complete extermination very appealing. If this is the case, then it goes without saying that Colonel Chivington's attack on Black Kettle's camp at Sand Creek must have brought a smile to his face. Yet, despite Sherman's all-out search-and-destroy attitude against *all Indians*, it was clear that the US government had to do something, as settlers were being attacked and killed, Kansas Pacific Railroad construction crews were being harassed, and warriors were attacking and burning the various mail stations along the way. Indeed, all of the stations stretching through the Smoky Hill route—Downer, White Rock, Stormy Hollow, Lookout, Big Creek, and Forsythe's Creek Station—were all under threat of attack.

The march would consist of units of cavalry, infantry, and artillery, and would assemble from the various forts in the area. Custer, leading his Seventh Cavalry, would be the lightning rod of the expedition, ready to give chase if needed, and always leading the slower infantry and artillery units. Custer's direct superior and actual commanding officer of the Seventh Cavalry, Colonel Andrew Jackson Smith, was part of this expedition, and was an old hand at fighting Indians. Commanding the entire expedition out of Fort Leavenworth was General Winfield Scott Hancock, a hero of the Civil War, whose nickname during those years was Hancock the Superb. Hancock's personality, disposition, and policy toward the Indians could best be described as having one's hand on the gun with a finger rubbing the trigger. It's not that he absolutely wanted war with the Sioux and Cheyenne, but his mission was undoubtedly punitive, and if the Indians didn't like what he had to say, the killing would begin. This left very little wiggle room for negotiation with even the friendly Indians. In Hancock's mind, the Indians were going onto the reservation or into their graves. He had the support of General Sherman and others back in Washington who saw what a tremendous economic gain either outcome would produce once the Indian "problem" was solved. It was a harsh policy from the president downward, and it was up to the military to make it happen.

The command moved in a southwesterly direction, their first goal making camp at Fort Harker some seventy-five miles from Fort Riley. Harker, unlike the appealing stone and wood buildings of Fort Riley, was little more than a small collection of single-story mud-and-log huts which had weeds growing atop the flat roofs.[3] The troops didn't stay long, and the command pushed past Fort Harker and on to Fort Larned at Pawnee Fork, along the Arkansas River, where Hancock would make his base camp and prepare to meet with chiefs from an Indian encampment some thirty miles away. Here, the inexperienced Indian fighter would test the waters to see what the intentions of the Plains Indians were, and what his next response should be. The US government was attempting to keep the Southern Cheyenne, Kiowa, and Arapaho tribes on reservations south of the Arkansas River, while corralling the Sioux north of the Platte River. This looked good on paper, and if successful, would in theory allow for the unmolested travel of whites throughout much of Kansas and Nebraska[4] and guarantee the safety of all concerned. The only problem with this, of course, was that it was forced upon them. While many Indians were willing to go along with it, however bitter it was for them to do so, many of their braves were not. It didn't take a large war party to race from spot to spot across the prairie, kill white people, burn coach stations, or disrupt the Kansas Pacific Railroad and to create a great deal of havoc. Indeed, the Indians had become very adept at conducting these lightning raids and then quickly disappearing beyond the horizon. The army was determined to put a stop to it all.

It is worth noting here that just as the plan to corral the Indians was rife with problems, so, too, was the army's ability to deal with situations both within and without its control. This made life both difficult and dangerous for the common trooper. For example, the surgeon traveling with the Hancock Expedition, Dr. Isaac Coates, describes how frostbite was a major problem from the moment the command departed Fort Riley. This was due to the lack of proper clothing, and the inability of the army to recognize the severity of the weather on the Great Plains.[5] Apparently, the rate of medical casualties was far above that found in regular army life, and could have, for the most part, been completely averted had the soldiers been supplied with adequate clothing for the winter months and equipped with lighter summer uniforms for the hot campaigns to come. Had this occurred, the number of men succumbing in the summer to heat exhaustion from the heavy Civil War uniforms they were forced to button up every morning would have been far less.[6]

Another frustrating condition was the supplying of weapons to the Indians. According to Custer, the problem was rampant, and an indicator of how foolish and counterproductive the government could be. Of course, this lack of sensible decision-making by a governmental body is rather timeless, as egregious and foolish decisions have always been made, and while the nature of the absurdity changes, the absurdity itself does not. After writing about the bow and arrow, the lance, tomahawk, knife, and other traditional weapons of the people of the Plains, Custer writes:

> *In addition to these weapons . . . each one was supplied with either a breech-loading rifle or revolver, sometimes with both—the latter obtained through the wise foresight and strong love of fair play which prevails in the Indian Department, which, seeing that its wards are determined to fight, is equally determined that there shall be no advantage taken, but that the two sides shall be armed alike; proving, too, in this manner the wonderful liberality of our Government, which not only is able to furnish its soldiers with the latest improved style of breech-loaders . . . and willing to give the same pattern of arms to their common foe. The only difference is, that the soldier, if he loses his weapon, is charged double price for it; while to avoid making any such charge against the Indian, his weapons are given him without conditions attached.*[7]

Like a bitter pill which is hard to swallow, the irony of the Plains Indians being equipped with weapons by the same government that has now ordered their subjugation was aggravating beyond reason, and yet the army was powerless to stop it.

The Indian encampment (they were in the area to hunt buffalo, as the beasts were plentiful in the region), occupied mostly by Sioux and Cheyenne, was very wary of Hancock, and they didn't like that such a large number of troops was so close by. Naturally, they didn't trust the motivations of the army, but they also understood that to turn a deaf ear toward them would ensure an open conflict would quickly break out. They would negotiate with the white man, that much was certain. The cultural gulf between the two, however, would engender problems from the start, and Hancock would meet his opposition with force at the slightest provocation (real or imagined). The Indians were under no illusion as to their fate if the plans of the whites came to fruition.

Having arrived at Fort Larned on April 7, Hancock instructed Indian agent Edward Wynkoop to seek out the chiefs for a conference at the fort. Wynkoop, along with another Indian agent, Jesse H. Leavenworth, were viewed by the army as little better than the Indians they served and entirely corrupt in their dealings with both the Indians and their own people. Still, they were the chosen go-betweens, and at least while working with Hancock, they delivered to the army their best guesses as to the Indians' intentions. Wynkoop's central message was that the army, displayed in such large numbers, was frightening the Indians, which, given the events of the recent slaughter at Sand Creek, was understandable. That said, the chiefs promised to come to the fort for peace talks.

The meeting was scheduled for April 10, but a snowstorm left eight inches on the ground, so the talks were postponed until the next day. The next day, however, brought a herd of buffalo close to the Indians, who deemed a hunt more important than the meeting and delayed the peace council until April 12. This did not please Hancock at all, as it was difficult for him (or any other officer, for that matter) to believe that a buffalo hunt was important enough to delay an appointment with the army. As such, he made the decision that should the Indians once again fail to show up for talks, the army would break camp and travel to the vicinity of the village, some thirty miles from Larned. While the Plains tribes were no doubt stalling for time for whatever reason, they did not want Hancock moving his soldiers any closer to the main village, as this would be seen as a sign of aggression. Because of this, a delegation of Indians came to see Hancock on the evening of April 11.

Custer was able to observe the Indians up close for the first time, and despite the urgency of the meeting, he writes: "Later in the evening, two chiefs of the Dog Soldiers, a band composed of the most warlike and troublesome Indians on the Plains, chiefly made up of Cheyenne, visited our camp. . . . [T]hey were accompanied by a dozen warriors."[8] A council fire was built, but before the proceedings could begin, the Indians requested dinner. After they had eaten, they spent additional time smoking their pipes before signaling they were ready to talk. The Indians' interpreter and agent were also present.

Along with Hancock, all of the officers were in attendance, and the Indians were quite impressed with the uniforms of "the few artillery officers who were present in all the glory of red horsehair plumes, aigulets, etc. The chiefs seemed puzzled to determine whether these insignia designated chieftains or medicine men."[9] Once the participants were ready to address the business at hand, Hancock began by saying he had come in peace and that he had no desire to make war with them. He outlined what the United States expected of them, and also expressed his disappointment that so few chiefs had come to the meeting. He told them of his intentions to move the camp in the morning and come to the Indian village. This did not sit well with the Indians, and even the advice of the Indian agent—that such a move would instill fear in the village—did nothing to sway Hancock from his plan. Yet Hancock had a point; you couldn't say that the arrival of two chiefs and a dozen warriors marked a consensus among all of the tribes. Chief Tall Bull, watching Hancock while listening to the interpreter, spoke up about the "scarcity of the buffaloes, his love for the white man, and the usual hint," Custer said, "that a donation in the way of refreshments would be highly acceptable." Finished with frivolity, Tall Bull then put some meat on the bones of his comments when he told Hancock that "he would have nothing new to say at the village."[10] If Tall Bull believed this would alter the army's course, it did not. In the morning the command would be on the move. Meanwhile, the Indians made plans of their own.

The command covered approximately twenty-one miles on their march that first day out of Larned, which meant there was still a buffer of some fourteen miles between the Indian village and the US Army. During the day, Custer said, the Indians could be seen on the horizon, watching their progress. Custer also noted large plumes of smoke rising in the direction of the village. Later Hancock would learn that a group of warriors, in an attempt to protect their people, had set fire to the prairie in the vicinity of the village, in hopes of diverting the army.[11] Clearly, the Plains Indians were becoming nervous, and more-stringent measures would need to be taken.

Just before the troopers arrived at the location where they would make camp, several chiefs and a band of warriors joined them for talks. Representing the Sioux was Chief Pawnee Killer, while Chief White Bull spoke for the Cheyenne. No matter their sincerity, in retrospect, this "meeting" was little more than a stalling tactic which would allow their people to make preparations for flight should that be necessary. When the chiefs left the following morning before dawn, they were supposed to return by 9:00 a.m. with a delegation of leaders that would satisfy Hancock. By 9:30, Bear Bull arrived at Hancock's headquarters and announced that the chiefs were, in fact, on their way, but that it would take some time for the party to arrive. This was not going to work for Hancock, who already had his suspicions concerning their true intentions. Washing his hands of such foolishness, the general gave the order to march. By 11:00 a.m., the army was mobile and heading toward the Indian village.

Custer, having remarked during the Civil War on the beauty of cavalry charges—the sabers glistening in the sunlight and scenes of approaching carnage—would, for the first time, experience the brightly arrayed warriors of the Plains. After having gone only several miles toward the village, Custer said they "witnessed one of the finest and most imposing military displays, prepared according to the Indian art of war. . . . It was nothing more nor less than an Indian line of battle drawn directly across our line of march. . . . Most of the Indians were mounted; all were bedecked in their brightest colors, their heads crowned with the brilliant war bonnet, their lances bearing the crimson pennant, bows strung, and quivers full of barbed arrows."[12]

At this time the army, cavalry, and artillery fanned out to their combat positions, ready to meet the threat, a sight that must have been intimidating to the warriors. Custer mentions in his writings that the cavalrymen drew their sabers, and as he recalled such exciting situations during the Civil War, he noted "the command was given to draw sabre. As the bright blades flashed from their scabbards into the morning sunlight . . . a most beautiful and wonderfully interesting sight was spread out before and around us. . . ."[13] Here again is the boyish aspect of Custer coming to the fore, as he delights in the sights of military display, in this case one that was quickly edging toward a bloody and violent conclusion. But as Custer gazed upon his men as they clasped their weapons and waited for the order to charge, a parley between the opposing forces occurred. The warrior Roman Nose, along with Chief Pawnee Killer and others, rode out to meet Hancock under a white flag, and violence was temporarily averted. Hancock made it very clear that if the Indians wanted war, he would give it to them. The Indians, sizing up the obvious disadvantages of attacking the army at that time, declared they desired only peace. This too was agreeable to the general, who then informed them of his plans to approach the village for talks, to which the party reluctantly agreed.

That evening, before the sun had set on the western sky, the command watched as the smoke rose from the tepees, seemingly indicating normal activity with the Indian families. Unbeknownst to them, however, it was just another ruse, for at that very moment the Indians were departing, leaving their lodges, blankets, buffalo robes, and other creature comforts behind so they could make an escape. This shows how much they feared that the army would attack the village, overwhelm it, and kill all of the men, women, and children. Even though everything looked calm to Custer, he contemplated the various challenges awaiting them in the days ahead and how Hancock would rise to meet those challenges. He wouldn't have to wait long.

Early the following morning, Custer was awakened with an order to mount the cavalry and surround the village, as Hancock now believed quite correctly that the Indians had departed. Accompanying Custer was an interpreter whose wife lived in the village. As the troops carefully and quietly surrounded the tepees, Custer, along with the interpreter and one of his good friends, Lieutenant Myles Moylan, crept on all fours toward a particular tepee. Pistol in hand, Custer was nervous at the thought of entering the lodge in case it was still occupied. The interpreter called out but received no answer, and told Custer he believed it could be a trap. Touching his ear to the outside of the deerskin structure, Custer heard no sounds at all. After a moment, he entered the lodge, pistol barrel first, and found it completely deserted.

Indeed, the entire village was empty, except for an old man, a couple of squaws, and a terrified and babbling white girl that Custer believed was perhaps as young as eight. Although she appeared to have been traumatized by her entire experience with the Indians, it was the raping she'd had to endure by some of the younger warriors as the village was breaking camp that had thrown her into a terrified state of mind. As Custer related in a letter to Libbie, "Dr. Coates and I found a little girl, not more than eight or nine . . . almost insensible, covered with blood. When able to talk she said, 'Those Indian men did me bad . . .' Woe to them if I overtake them. The chances of this, however, are slight, once they are forewarned."[14] That Custer would have killed these men if he'd been able to apprehend them is without question. If they had survived the battle, and had Custer been able to determine the actual culprits, they surely would have been executed on the spot. Beyond the corralling and the punishment of these rapists, the Indians were an elusive entity as a whole. Their ability to strike, flee, and disappear over the horizon was second to none. They were also very angry about being driven out of their village.

The Indians had left almost all of their personal belongings behind, including their rugs, blankets, tepees, and cooking pots. Some of the Indians had removed large pieces of deerskin from their lodges to provide families with temporary shelter during their escape. Still, it must have been terribly frustrating for the Sioux and Cheyenne to jettison some three hundred lodges because of what the soldiers might do.

It was April 15, and Custer and his cavalry were ordered to give chase. Accompanying them was a detachment of Delaware Indians, as well as civilian scouts, chief among them the famous James B. Hickok, better known as "Wild Bill." General Hancock, apparently believing the Indians might return, placed a guard around the village to protect it from scavengers. Although it was an honorable thing to do, it does seem a bit odd that he would consider even for a moment the possibility of their return. His mind would soon change on the matter.

As Custer set out across the Plains, the Indians, already traveling light, were discarding other essentials (like lodge poles) which were weighing them down. The command, try as they might, were unable to close the gap, as night was falling. The Delaware Indians did see some small bands of Indians off in the distance, and also noticed the exchanging of smoke signals as they communicated with each other. The next day's "chase" would be as uneventful as the first with respect to the overtaking and capturing of fleeing Indians. Custer would, however, place himself in one of the most precarious positions he would ever find himself in, and it was only chance and circumstance that would deliver him from the vagaries of his actions. In other words, Custer found himself in the wrong place at the right time, and as such, was not destroyed.

Despite the fact that George Custer had led men into battle countless times and understood the need for orderly command and structure, once again his boyish nature got the better of him. Having broken away from the column to chase antelope some two miles from the command, Custer galloped after them until he had no idea where he was in relation to the column. At the same moment when he should have been concerned about being lost in the middle of Indian country, he spotted a black speck on the horizon. Immediately his instincts told him that the grandest animal on the Great Plains—the buffalo—was grazing alone, just waiting to be attacked. The temptation was greater than he could stand. In an instant, Custer was galloping across the prairie on his first buffalo hunt. Having caught up with the bison, Custer chased him, running side by side and laughing out loud, he was so excited. He also admitted that although he had ample opportunity to shoot the animal, he was having such a good time that he couldn't bring himself to do it.

When Custer noticed the buffalo breathing hard after a several-mile run, he decided to end it. He pointed his pistol and prepared to fire. At the same moment, the animal took its furry horned head and attempted to gore Custer's horse. This caused Custer to grab the reins with both hands, and in doing so, he accidently squeezed the trigger. The subsequent blast sent a bullet into the back of the horse's head, killing it instantly. Later, Custer spoke of it in almost humorous terms, while at the same time fully understanding what dire circumstances he had placed himself in: "Running at full speed, [the horse] fell dead in the course of his leap. Quick as thought I disengaged myself from the stirrups and found myself whirling through the air over and beyond the head of my horse."[15] Custer expected to be attacked by the beast, but unlike Custer, who was out for blood during the hunt, the animal just wanted to be left alone.

Standing in the midst of the prairie, a dead horse at his feet and armed only with a pistol, Custer considered the possibility of a nasty encounter with Indians. He also wondered how and if the command would find him. Using field glasses, he set off in the direction he believed might offer some clue toward finding his way back, and after a time, spotted through the binoculars the telltale sign of dust rising into the air which meant that something—humans or animals—were heading his way. To his relief, as he scrutinized the situation through his field glasses, it became clear the shapes were human, and then the unmistakable sight of the cavalry guidon came into view. He would later write that he believed the distance he'd walked from his dead horse to where the troops discovered him was either three or four miles. "Custer's Luck" had saved him again.

As for the Sioux and Cheyenne, they were beyond the reach of the soldiers, having split off into many directions. Their answer to being driven from their village was to attack the various stagecoach stations as they traveled north, killing employees and burning the buildings to the ground. Things were heading toward all-out war, but it would be for the most part a war of their choosing. The elusive warriors of the Great Plains would strike yet another Fetterman-like blow later that summer against their enemy in a war that rarely offered mercy. Custer, in a letter to Libbie, spoke truthfully about the reasons why an Indian war needed to be averted. Should one begin, however, he believed a war of extermination was the way to proceed. As Custer would soon learn, extermination has many faces and can take many forms—and one face lay just around the corner.

CHAPTER 6

Take No Prisoners

The Hancock Expedition did not prove to be the panacea the United States had intended. It would, however, plod along and provide two very big negatives, and Custer would play a part in both events. Custer's boyish nature, propelling him forward in the same reckless spirit that had driven him to chase that lone buffalo, would play a major role in one of these. And while the threat of death was not in the equation for this particular chase toward what Custer wanted, it nearly destroyed his military career, and certainly derailed it for a time.

Soon after Custer had rejoined the command after accidentally killing his horse, it was learned that the Indians were attacking the stagecoach stations along the Smoky Hill route, killing the workers and setting fire to the buildings. Each station, spaced some ten to fifteen miles apart, was manned by several employees. When word began reaching the stations that were still in one piece, the workers fled to surrounding stations for safety; they believed their larger numbers could aid them in mounting a proper defense. When Custer sent back word to General Hancock as to what the fleeing Indians were up to, he destroyed the village he was formerly protecting. That the Sioux and Cheyenne would respond in this way seemed a bit of a surprise to him, but it shouldn't have. The ghastly destruction of Black Kettle's camp at Sand Creek had made an indelible mark on the tribes, and the army was seeing the results even now. In this war of cultures, mercy and goodwill toward your enemy, even when one had the upper hand, was sadly lacking.

According to Custer's memoirs, now that the Indians were conducting raids, the "principal theater of military operations during the summer would be between the Smoky Hill and Platte Rivers."[1] These military operations would always be focused on the subjugation of Indians, hopefully peacefully, but violently if necessary, so that a return to their reservations and an upholding of their portions of the treaty would be assured. It is also important to note that the Indians continually denied responsibility for their actions. Whenever the US government pressed them for answers concerning the irrefutable depredations the Indians were committing against the whites, they heard "We didn't do it!" It was always another tribe responsible for the raids, or another faction committing the murders, and so forth. It was passing the buck in its most egregious form. And the Indian agents, who were in fact knowledgeable as to the true identity of the culprits, kept silent so as not to disturb the lucrative business deals they were conducting. In truth, a segment of each of the Plains tribes was involved in acts of war against the United States. So while the Sioux and Cheyenne were now in open warfare, the army was determined to placate the Kiowa and Arapaho tribes.

Ready for war but showing a great willingness for peace, General Hancock welcomed chiefs Satanta, Kicking Bird, and Lone Wolf of the Kiowa tribe, and Little Raven and Yellow Bear from the Arapaho, to a meeting at Fort Dodge. Satanta, a brave warrior and chief to his people, was a skilled orator and would use these skills to great effect during his meeting with Hancock. Of course, everything he said was a lie meant to calm the fears of his enemy, and in this he succeeded. It's almost comical that anyone present believed him. Even Custer could not help but see the irony of it all: "So effective and convincing was the oratorical effort of Satanta, that at the termination of his address the department commander and staff presented him with the uniform coat, sash, and hat of a major general. In return for this compliment Satanta, within a few weeks after, attacked the post at which the conference was held, arrayed in his new uniform."[2] The gullibility of the whites must have seemed very strange to Satanta.

By late April Custer and the Seventh Cavalry would be ensconced at Fort Hays, awaiting orders. Custer was not sure where General Hancock had landed or the exact whereabouts of his immediate superior officer and actual commander of the regiment, General Smith. But he knew where his dear Libbie was, and he was growing more homesick for her with each passing day. In a letter dated May 2, 1867, Custer wrote: "Come as soon as you can. 'Whom God hath joined . . .' I did not marry you for you to live in one house, me in another. One bed shall accommodate us both."[3] Elizabeth Custer, along with her friend, Anna, and their cook, Eliza, would finally reach Fort Hays in late May, just before Custer departed on another campaign to corral the Indians.

In a letter penned just a day earlier, Custer tells of a buffalo hunt that he and some of the officers had participated in, and the inevitable result from such a "sport": "Yesterday Captains Hamilton and Benteen, and Lts. Moylan and Nolen and Drs. Coates, Lippincott with half a dozen men went buffalo hunting, intending to return about 5:00 p.m. Captain Benteen shot his favorite horse dead, also a large buffalo dog belonging to 'E Company' just as it had the buffalo by the nose. The dog will recover. . . ."[4] True to form for those making mad dashes across the Plains, several men got lost and wouldn't find their way back to Fort Hays until the following day.

On yet another buffalo hunt, Custer tells of riding some five miles while chasing his prey when his horse, loaned to him by Captain Louis McLane Hamilton (a grandson of Alexander Hamilton), began to give out. Custer, believing the animal was on the verge of collapsing, quickly dismounted so as not to be violently thrown to the ground once again. "In doing so," Custer writes, "my pistol accidently discharged into his free shoulder, entirely disabling him." Thus ended another buffalo hunt for Custer. He also conveyed to Libbie that in total, seven buffalo were successfully hunted and killed that day by other members of the command.

Bad weather had prevented Custer from departing Fort Hays on the schedule he'd envisioned, and his mood was deteriorating very quickly. Indeed, his behavior had become so foul that his actions began to replicate the harsh treatment that his troops had had to endure in Texas and Louisiana. When it was discovered that six men from companies E and H had gone to the post (one half-mile from camp) to purchase canned fruit so as to possibly stave off the scurvy now ravaging the soldiers at the fort, without permission, Custer ordered their heads shaved. Not all of their head, mind you, but only half, so they would appear freakish and ridiculous, and obviously humiliated. Once this was accomplished, they were marched around camp and then confined to their quarters. It was a mean-spirited act, and one that would not win Custer any friends.

On the contrary, Captain Albert Barnitz, an able officer of the Seventh Cavalry, easily recognized Custer's flawed personality and spoke eloquently of the events in a letter dated May 15, 1867, to his wife Jennie back east: "Things are becoming very unpleasant here. General Custer is very injudicious in his administration, and spares no effort to render himself generally obnoxious. . . . He is the most complete example of a petty tyrant that I have ever seen. You would be filled with utter amazement if I were to give you a few instances of his cruelty to the men, and discourtesy to the officers. . . ."[5] Barnitz would always see George Custer through the prism of these egregious faults as a commander, for such behavior, in his view, was the complete opposite of what a good leader should strive for.

And herein lies the chasm that would become so evident in the Seventh Cavalry, where those supporting Custer (family and close friends) couldn't see, or turned a blind eye toward, the sometimes-appalling actions of Custer toward his men and fellow officers. Those outside this inner circle could quite plainly see the inconsistencies, slights, and outright hypocritical abuses of power that Custer would often dish out to others, while at the same time thinking nothing of committing infractions himself. Although Barnitz had originally liked and respected Custer, the passage of time and his association with him would soon change his opinion.

Another officer clearly outside the good graces of Custer was the very capable soldier, Captain Frederick Benteen. Benteen, whose disposition toward his men and fellow officers was nothing like that of the boy general, would grow to despise Custer and would go down in the history of the Seventh Cavalry as being Custer's biggest detractor. Not without his own faults, Benteen could nevertheless see right through Custer and was very unforgiving of his poor behavior.

⸻

The Seventh Cavalry, temporarily without Custer but under the command of Major Wickliffe Cooper, would again hit the trail in the hunt for the Indians on the first of June. (On a sad note, Cooper, a good and capable officer, would commit suicide in a matter of weeks due to his struggle with alcohol, leaving a loving wife and unborn child.) Projecting a force of some 350 men and at least twenty wagons carrying provisions, the command began moving north, with their first goal that of pressing toward Fort McPherson. Thus far the campaign had been rather uneventful, but that would change in the days ahead. Custer, desiring to spend one more night with the woman he loved, set out to join the command just after midnight, taking with him only two soldiers, the scout William Comstock, and four Delaware guides. It was highly risky, guided only by moonlight, but Custer rode all night and caught up with the Seventh encamped in a valley some twenty miles from Fort Hays. He arrived just as reveille was being sounded, which meant he and his companions would be joining the day's march without any sleep. This wouldn't bother the boy general, whose physical stamina was nothing short of legendary.

Custer's push north toward Fort McPherson would be uneventful. A large Sioux and Cheyenne war party was known to be out raiding, but he didn't know where they were. Thus far they had managed to avoid contact with their blue-coated hunters. Upon arrival, Custer's orders were to remain at the fort until General Sherman arrived, which would occur in the next several days, so he moved the command to a spot about twelve miles away, putting down tents along the clear, cool waters of the Platte River. The Indians, once again proving their skill at being elusive, were wise in carefully choosing their time of battle. Custer would later write (again, in almost humorous terms) of this distinction for the Plains tribes, which must have provided considerable frustration for the regiment: "... we again set out in search of Indians ... [who] are sought after so frequently and found so seldom, except when not wanted...."[6]

Custer, on the other hand, commanded such a large force, and had absolute confidence in their ability to defeat the Plains warriors wherever and whenever they were destined to meet, that battle at any time or place was fine with him. He wasn't worried in the least about an encounter. That said, he preferred peace (perhaps so he could return to Libbie), and he would enter again into a parley of sorts with Pawnee Killer and a party of Indians who arrived along the Platte River about the same time as the Seventh Cavalry. It was Custer's hope that by convincing Pawnee Killer of the army's benign intentions, he and all the Indians in the area would plant their villages by the fort and remain at peace with the whites. Of course, Custer was under no illusions as to the likelihood of preventing war with the Indians, but peace was preferable when it came to plans for westward expansion, and everyone knew it. The talks with the chiefs would lead to no agreements, and despite the usual proclamations from the Indians concerning their peaceful intentions, Custer knew these words were nothing more than lies. Pawnee Killer even went so far as to ask Custer about the army's intentions upon leaving Fort McPherson, and in what direction they might be traveling. Custer refused to answer, but gave them the obligatory gifts of coffee and sugar as a sign of goodwill. A full-fledged Indian war was in the making, and Custer knew it.

After restocking supplies, the Seventh Cavalry headed west along the trail to Fort Sedgwick, located in Colorado Territory, with a keen eye toward telltale signs of movement from any Sioux and Cheyenne war party that might be in the area. However, Custer then led the column in a southwesterly direction toward the fork of the Republican River. This was an area where he fully expected to locate Indians, as the army was well aware that several war parties were traversing this portion of western Kansas, northern Nebraska, and the adjacent Colorado Territory. It was just a question of finding the parties, or perhaps, of the Indians finding them.

Within days of the command leaving Fort McPherson, they found themselves encamped along the Republican River. Early in the morning, lying in his tent, Custer was in that twilight state—not asleep and not fully awake, but certainly untroubled. In an instant, the loud blast of an army carbine split the air, and Custer jumped to his feet. He knew it had come from a picket at the far end of the camp. At the same moment, Tom Custer, officer of the day, stuck his head in the tent, shouting "They are here!"[7] and then he left. Of course, no explanation was needed as to who *they* were. Clad only in a robe, the shoeless and hatless George Custer grabbed his Spencer carbine and ran toward the sound of the firing.

The Indians, numbering some three hundred, were quickly beaten back and retreated to a hill not a mile distant. Custer, desiring to know who it was that had attacked, showed an incredible amount of restraint and sent a trooper to ride out a short distance and signal to the Indians for a parley. This was agreed upon by the chiefs, and Custer, taking six officers, a bugler, and an interpreter, met the Indians at the river, which was, at that time of year, little more than a stream. On Custer's side of the river, it was merely grass, but the opposite bank had willow trees and places where one could easily hide.

After dismounting, the chiefs removed their leggings and crossed the stream. As they approached, Custer was surprised to see Pawnee Killer, who was, in fact, the head chief of the group. He had made proclamations of peace only weeks before, and was rewarded by the government with offerings of sugar and coffee. His appearance sent unspoken ripples of anger through the gathering of officers. According to Custer, as soon as Pawnee Killer and the others had crossed the stream, they threw up their hands and said "How" and the parley began. Custer had wisely placed his bugler some distance in the rear and informed him that should Custer signal, he was to sound the alarm so that the entire command could begin the gallop toward them.

It would not be a productive meeting. Each side was after information as to the upcoming activities the other was planning. Custer believed (quite correctly) that Pawnee Killer and his people, despite their attempt to murder them only moments before, should move their village close to the army encampment. That way he could keep an eye on them, offering at least the facade of friendship, and this closeness would hinder the Indians from attacking two detachments of troops that were even then conducting operations out on the prairie. Custer was so suspicious of the current intentions of these Indians that he did not remove his hand from his revolver the entire time he was involved in the talk. He had good reason to be suspicious, as Pawnee Killer had every intention of murdering the little band of soldiers before the conclusion of the meeting.

Just as the talks were about to end, Custer noticed a young warrior, fully armed, emerge from the trees on the other side of the river. As the Indian began to cross, Custer didn't give a lot of thought to it. But as a second young brave came out of the trees, he knew Pawnee Killer had something special in mind. Almost immediately, two other warriors made their way over toward the group. Outwardly, all greeted Custer and his men with the traditional raising of the hands and the uttering of that singular word. When Custer pointed out to Pawnee Killer that he was breaking their agreed-upon rules for the talks—that they should be between the seven chiefs and Custer and his six officers—the chief tried to assuage their fears. Now outnumbered eleven to seven, Custer made it clear that no other warriors were to cross over. But as the talk was resumed, another party came out of the tall grass and trees. As Custer recalled, he stopped to once again remind "Pawnee Killer of the stipulations of our agreement, and that while we had regarded ours faithfully, he had disregarded his...."[8]

Custer then pointed out to the chief that his bugler was standing at a safe distance from them. Custer warned Pawnee Killer that if even one more warrior attempted to cross over, he would give the signal, and the bugler would alert the entire command, bringing the full weight of the Seventh Cavalry to bear. This was enough to thwart the plans of Pawnee Killer, who quickly held up his hand and motioned that no more braves should cross the river.

After this, the talk was suspended. Custer understood that nothing of value had been gained. True, he knew the identity of his attackers, but that was all. As Pawnee Killer rejected Custer's offer to bring his village close to their camp, Custer said he would move his soldiers to their village. This did not sit well with the Indians. The Indians, amazed at the gullibility of their white enemies, actually had the audacity to ask for sugar, coffee, and ammunition before they departed. This time Custer refused their request, and both parties retreated to safer ground. The chiefs and the handful of warriors crossed back over, mounted their ponies, and made haste to join the main body of Indians who were now about two miles in the distance. Custer vainly attempted to have the Seventh Cavalry follow them, but the swifter Indian ponies made that all but impossible.

In truth, despite his good intentions, Custer would not have succeeded no matter what he had tried. The Indians were on the war path, and no one was safe. No amount of coaxing would have changed the minds of the Sioux and those allied with them who were out for white blood. It was clear they would parley to obtain information and gifts of food and ammunition, but nothing short of force would have caused them to back off now that the violence was in full swing. Communication being what it was in those days meant that wherever and whenever the Indians struck next, it would be some time before their activities would be generally known throughout the region. Such was the case with Lieutenant Lyman S. Kidder and his doomed platoon.

On June 29, General Sherman, headquartered at Fort Sedgwick, instructed Lieutenant Lyman S. Kidder, twenty-five years old and a Civil War veteran, to saddle up a platoon of troops and carry dispatches to Custer who was then (supposedly) still camped along the north fork of the Republican River. With a salute, Kidder wasted no time fulfilling his orders. The only problem was that Custer, who had grown antsy while encamped along the river, had decided to move the Seventh out to search for Indians. He had headed south into Kansas and then northwest into Colorado. Now, some have openly blamed Custer for this move, but it must be remembered that Sherman had given him a wide berth in his hunt for the marauding bands of Indians, and sitting along a riverbank does not constitute a hunt. The foul-up here was that Sherman was expecting Custer to put in for supplies at Sedgwick, but Custer, always one to do things his own way, had decided to send wagons to Fort Wallace for the needed food and munitions, and no one knew of this change of plans. (They would be attacked upon their return, but the Indians were repulsed.) Of course, the real reason behind Custer's plan to send wagons to Wallace was to pick up Libbie, under guard, and have her escorted safely to him—but Libbie was not there, as he would soon learn. She was still at Fort Riley. Although Custer had believed that she'd already made the journey from Riley to Wallace, he was thankful to learn she was still at Riley due to the eruption of hostilities.

In any event, when Custer reached Riverside Station, some forty miles west of Fort Sedgwick, and telegraphed the fort, he learned that Kidder was out looking for him along the Republican River. Knowing how hostile the country had become, Custer became concerned and immediately gave orders for a march east once again.

Making as good a time as was humanly possible, Custer's Seventh would retrace their steps with hopes that Kidder and his men had somehow managed to avoid the roving war parties. But this endless life in the saddle was beyond what many troopers could endure. They neither possessed Custer's stamina nor did they have at their disposal the fine thoroughbreds Custer was accustomed to riding. Because of this, desertions in the Western army were rampant, and such exhausting and physically debilitating expeditions as Custer was used to gave rise to even more bold daylight flights to freedom.

During one such instance, thirteen men were seen galloping across the prairie. Custer ordered Major Joel Elliott and his men to give chase. Custer had already given Elliott permission to kill them if necessary, and gunshots were soon heard, leaving those in camp no doubt as to the reason for the firing. One trooper was shot through the head and killed, and several of the fleeing soldiers were wounded. This action taken by Custer evidently made a great impression on would-be deserters, as they suddenly stopped running off, and what had been an ongoing problem was at least for the present time cured. Custer, who had first loudly denied medical care to the returning wounded, would later that evening give Dr. Isaac Coates permission to treat them.

But despite their valiant efforts, the Kidder party had already been destroyed. Upon reaching the area where Kidder and his men were last known to be searching, a trooper found the remains of a dead horse. Soon a trail was located revealing torn earth, indicating the heavy and fast-paced galloping of horses, and this led to a dry ravine along a creek bed where the mystery was solved: Lieutenant Lyman S. Kidder and his entire command had been killed, apparently in a running battle along Beaver Creek. It was a depressing discovery. True to form, the warriors had mutilated and scalped everyone except Kidder's Sioux scout, Red Bear. Several corpses had also been burned. The Kidder Massacre was the first event during the Hancock Expedition that would, rightly or wrongly, be permanently linked to George Custer.

The second Custer snafu would occur soon after, and would be born out of his typical attitude toward military rules and regulations—less stringent for him, more stringent for others. This is the outlook that he carried with him throughout his military career, and it would cost him dearly this time. The boy general was not finished acting out.

Unbeknownst to Custer, action had been taking place at Fort Wallace and the surrounding territory, with the fort being attacked twice—not a tactic in which Indians usually participated. In writing home to his wife, Albert Barnitz gave a detailed account of the fight, which also appeared in the July 27, 1867, issue of *Harper's Weekly*. In his letter, Barnitz describes the layout of the fort: "The post is handsomely situated on high ground about a quarter of a mile distant from the south fork of the Smoky, a small stream of pure, never-failing water, beyond which the prairie gradually rises for a distance of five miles, where the view is bounded by a range of magnificent bluffs, quite mountainous in appearance, and the summits of which are so clearly defined in the pure atmosphere of this climate that the head of an Indian could be readily seen if one should appear above the hills. . . ."[9] Barnitz had no worries concerning the stealthy attacks of the warriors, with their feathered heads silhouetted against the horizon, for now their foes were making war on them openly. When Custer and his Seventh arrived at Fort Wallace, it was in sorry shape. Depleted of men by the spread of cholera as well as from Indian attacks, its inability to receive supplies due to the constant threat of attack and the lack of communication between the commands made for a gloomy reception when the Seventh dismounted.

Now that a full-blown Indian war was igniting the prairie, Custer's ability to connect with Libbie was severely restricted. He had originally wanted her to join him at Wallace, but that hadn't happened, and as Custer now realized, such a journey could have been disastrous. Of necessity, she could not "campaign" with her Autie in the same manner she'd been accustomed to during the Civil War, following him around from camp to camp. Life on the Western frontier often required her to remain behind at whatever fort or camp Custer and his Seventh Cavalry were assigned. In this regard, if Custer was unable to join her, he might, if safety permitted, have her escorted to another post where he could rendezvous with his love for any number of days, or hours. Even so, it meant periods of long separation. It would be the drive to be with "his girl" that would temporarily lead the boy general away from the career he loved so much. In Custer's mind, Libbie had been safely awaiting his return while he was being exposed to danger as he sought the rebellious Plains Indians. But Libbie was battling dangers of her own.

Only days after Custer had joined the Seventh after his all-night moonlight gallop, Libbie, along with Jennie Barnitz and other soldier's wives, had endured two days of violent storms in their camp at Big Creek. Writing of her experience, Jennie Barnitz spoke of the frightful experience of June 7, 1867: "The lightning was chain & burst like rockets, & some said fairly hissed & fell like stars," and she declared the thunder "[m]uch heavier than cannonading."[10] The water started rising so quickly that Colonel Smith stuck his head into Jennie Barnitz's tent and yelled for her to hurry, as they needed to get to higher ground. At one point they believed a tornado was bearing down on them. Libbie Custer said she took comfort in the fact that they were all together, and if anything bad was going to happen to them, she was glad the "general" wasn't there to see it. Fortunately, even though tornadoes were prevalent on the Kansas prairie—something all residents were well aware of—they were not part of these storms, and despite the drowning of three troopers who were carried away in the flood, everyone else remained safe and secure. Soon after this, the women (including Libbie) were sent back to Fort Riley.[11]

The general couldn't wait to see Libbie, and the jumping-off point for his departure from the command was quickly approaching. No sooner had he arrived at Fort Wallace and discovered that Libbie had not made the trip, he made plans to mount up again and head east to Fort Harker. Having the captains of each of the six companies pick twelve of their best troopers and mounts, Custer would retain seventy-two men for this venture. The troops, no matter how good their mounts, were exceedingly exhausted from the ride to Wallace, and beginning a second jaunt was something they wanted no part of. But orders were orders. From Fort Hays, Custer would continue on to Fort Harker, where he would board a train for the remainder of the trip. But he would have to get past Colonel Smith first. His drive to see Libbie was reaching a boiling point, and it may have been fear and apprehension propelling him forward.

Apparently, one circulating story has it that Custer had received a letter from a fellow officer about the time Libbie had been spending with Lieutenant Thomas B. Weir and the possible problems arising from such a friendship. Of course, Custer could easily be thrown into a fit of jealousy, as was the case when he turned Libbie over to others at West Point while he visited with former professors during their brief stop at the academy after their wedding. But the thought of something happening which could very well result in physical contact between his wife and Weir was too much to bear and threatened to push him mentally over the edge. According to Frederick Benteen (who absolutely despised Custer, and no doubt took great pleasure recounting the story), when Custer confronted Weir, he threw him to the ground, and it ended with Weir practically begging for mercy. This seems a bit overdramatized, but if Weir felt he was being caught in the act (even if the relationship was never a sexual one), and he realized that his affections for Libbie had crossed the line (where he knew he had at least emotionally betrayed Custer), then it may be an accurate description of what happened between the two men. Where the actual truth resides in all of this is uncertain. What is not uncertain is that something improper was noticed by others concerning Weir and Libbie, and Custer was determined to stop it in its tracks.

It is interesting to note here that even a cursory reading of the letters exchanged by Libbie and George reveals a subtle attempt to invoke jealousy in the other party, however innocently they went about it. Perhaps it had its genesis in the stinging remarks of one, only to be answered by the offended party with similar stories. This could have gone on for some time without being openly spoken about when the two were finally together. But casual flirtation, however repugnant it may have appeared to them, was not the same as what Custer perceived here. In his mind it had become something far more, perhaps resulting in sexual relations. Despite whatever indiscretion had occurred between Libbie and the handsome and refined Thomas Weir, tongues would wag in the near future about a relationship he would have with a beautiful Indian woman.

In any event, Custer had a plan, and he wanted to fulfill it. Having blazed a trail from Forts Wallace to Hays, Custer would press on to Fort Harker, where he would board a train for Fort Riley. Upon his arrival at Harker, Custer chose his words carefully as he spoke to a very tired Colonel Smith between 2:00 and 3:00 a.m., after having the colonel awakened. Andrew Smith, who had spent many years in the saddle battling Confederates and Indians, was unusually good-natured and always strove to be civil with people. Custer, in an attempt to be evasive and reach Libbie, insinuated to Smith that he already had orders to proceed there. It was a lie—Custer knew it—yet Smith bid him a fond farewell.

Not only was it a lie, but it was a lie with consequences. Custer had no business at Fort Riley. His new orders, which he'd received only a short time before arriving at Harker, locked him into his command at Fort Wallace, and he was to operate between the Platte and Arkansas Rivers, looking for war parties. Custer, along with every other commander, officer, and trooper, was needed right there. Indeed, more expeditions awaited him, and the last thing the army wanted was for any officer to be shirking his duty and running home to his wife. Custer was also keenly aware of what a difficult time the army was having—not just locating Indians, but preventing them from killing and stealing at will. Indian attacks were never just about murder or removing the white man from their land. Their aim was to rid themselves of the white man while stealing from him all that he owned: horses, cattle, weapons and ammunition, food and clothing, and everything that could be used, sold, or bartered. The attempt of Pawnee Killer and his warriors to stampede and steal the horses of Custer's regiment the morning of the recent attack had quickly failed, thanks to the keen eye of the picket on guard. But on June 12, the Indians struck Fort Dodge and made off with all the horses belonging to Company A of the Seventh Cavalry. In an instant, the horse soldiers became foot soldiers—at least until they could secure more strong and dependable mounts. Stagecoach stations were being hit, railroad work came to a halt as workers were being attacked and killed, and settlers everywhere were at risk every minute of the day.

Add to this the overburdened military—a force that was working hard to stem the tide of violence, but had thus far been almost wholly unsuccessful at doing so—and you have a recipe for disaster. Custer was fully aware of the chaotic nature of the Plains at this time. Things had become so unstable that the governor of Kansas, Samuel Crawford, was extremely dissatisfied with the lack of progress the army was making, and offered to raise a cavalry regiment from the citizens of the state—an obvious slap in the face to General Sherman, of course, as everyone was looking to him for the answers. But Sherman, having grown suspicious of such a cavalry squadron being raised from the general population, due to what terrible things Chivington's men had done at Sand Creek, would only use them in the direst of circumstances. Yet by July 1, the crusty old warrior would relent and grant Crawford his wish, allowing him to form six to eight companies of troops. And while it would be unfair to accuse Custer of not caring about all of this, his mind at the time was filled with Libbie, and getting to his wife superseded all other interests.

Early the next morning, however, a clearheaded Smith came to the conclusion that Custer had no authority to visit his wife at Riley and wired him to return at once. Custer asked for a short delay, but Smith told him no, adding that he was to report immediately to him at Fort Harker. According to Colonel Smith, Custer, through no fault of his own, could not catch a train until July 21. When he did show up with Libbie and all their things, Smith, having already conferred with General Hancock, placed Custer under arrest.[12] George Armstrong Custer was about to suffer the indignity of a court-martial.

CHAPTER 7

Consequences and Restoration

Custer's actions were considered outrageous by everyone except Custer. Bad as it looked, though, no one who knew the boy general wanted him removed from duty, as his talent as a leader of cavalrymen was sorely needed. The Western theater was not just igniting; in the minds of many, it was out of control, with the Indians dictating the terms as to how the war would be conducted. Colonel Smith carried an emotional and mental burden just trying to meet the needs of the hard-hit area, and Custer's departure was not sitting well with the mild-mannered officer. Custer would come to believe that it was General Hancock who pressed Smith to push toward a court-martial.

Lieutenant General Ulysses S. Grant was responsible for deciding whether or not Custer was going to trial, and he gave the go-ahead on August 27, 1867. The trial, held at Fort Leavenworth, began on September 15 and would run for approximately three weeks. The charges against Custer were "Absence without leave from his command" and "Conduct to the prejudice of good order and military discipline."[1] The second charge stemmed from his wearing out of the horses during the forced marches, which of course was true. They could have added the wearing out of the men as well, but the troopers rebounded faster than their mounts.

At no time did Custer acknowledge the validity of the complaints against him. Although he continued to sidestep the issues, the excuses he gave for his actions did not hold up in court. Without calling these statements of Custer's lies, the record states: "The conclusion unavoidably reached . . . is that General Custer's anxiety to see his family at Fort Riley overcame his apprehension of the paramount necessity to obey orders . . . and that the excuses he offers for his acts of insubordination are *afterthoughts* [italics added]." They used the word *afterthoughts* to describe Custer's deception, but everyone knew they were lies. It is certain Custer believed he was correct in fleeing to Libbie. Whether it was born out of an overwhelming need to be with his wife or a desire to put a stop to a potential problem with Weir, Custer temporarily cast aside his role as commander and returned to his wife as quickly as possible. He drove man and beast nearly into the ground, and in doing so, exposed his command to dangers that were unnecessary. Although Custer accomplished his goal, it had a price attached to it.

At the end of the trial, Custer was convicted on both counts. A third charge, brought by Captain Robert West under the "Conduct prejudicial to good order and military discipline," sought to hammer Custer on the shooting down of the party of deserters by his order. Personally, West was angry that a soldier under his direct command, one Charles Johnson, had been shot in the head during the chase and had died soon thereafter. But desertions had been rampant, and while the deceased did not have the option of a fair military trial, he also refused to stop while being pursued and was part of the group that had fired on Major Elliott and the others as they approached them. This charge was rejected by the court. Having received no satisfaction from the military, West then brought charges of murder against Custer and William W. Cooke (the one who knocked Johnson from his saddle with a well-placed shot), but a civilian judge quickly found the charges unsubstantiated and dismissed the case. Custer, in turn, brought charges of drunkenness while on duty against West, and the resulting trial would leave Captain West convicted and suspended from duties for two months without pay. This, perhaps, was the only bright spot in the fallout from Custer's dash home. West's aggressiveness did not bode well for the enraged captain.

Custer's punishment for this dereliction of duty was removal from command, having his rank suspended, and losing one year's pay. It was a bitter pill for the boy general to swallow. He had sacrificed so much for the army and had placed himself in danger countless times. Yet, he had broken the rules and had refused to acknowledge it, believing that denial was the best defense. This, too, was the boy emerging in Custer once again: The rules were meant for others, and apparently he believed he deserved a free pass. It was a difficult time in the lives of the Custers. Libbie summed up their feelings best when she wrote: "When he ran the risk of a court-martial in leaving Wallace he did it expecting the consequences . . . and we are quite determined not to live apart again, even if he leaves the army otherwise so delightful to us."[2]

Although exiled from his life's work, Custer was at least with the most important person in his world. Accepting the kind offer of Major General Philip Sheridan to stay at his Fort Leavenworth headquarters while he was away (Custer was always his favorite officer), the Custers were able to spend quality time together and perhaps iron out any differences they may have had. Although it's certain Custer inwardly brooded over this inglorious outcome, he would do his time out of the saddle patiently, waiting for the future. At the age of twenty-eight, he had accomplished more than most men do in a lifetime of military service. But thus far, service in the West had not been very kind to Custer. It had not provided him with the almost constant successes the Civil War had handed him. He did not know what the future held, but his hunger for military life and adventure was in his blood. No matter what thoughts he may have briefly entertained during this low period, they were not of any real significance. Custer had lived as a soldier all of his adult life, and it was as much a part of him as breathing. He knew it and Libbie knew it. And furthermore, the top brass of the army knew it as well.

— ⋗⋖ —

By the summer of 1868, the Custers were once again in Monroe, Michigan. During his exile, Custer had plenty of time with Libbie and their friends, to do what he pleased. He used this period to pen his Civil War memoirs, and of course, he waited. When the request for his help came from Sheridan, it was more than Custer expected: "Generals Sherman,

Sully and myself, have asked for you, and I hope the application will be successful. Can you come at once? Eleven companies of your regiment will move about the 1st of October against the hostile Indians. . . ."[3] Custer's life of soldiering would continue after all. This must have been a special moment for Custer, as it dulled the sting he'd received ten months earlier.

No real progress had been made since Custer's banishment to the sidelines. Looking to be innovative, Sheridan had decided that, along with what the conventional army was doing to hinder the Plains Indians, Major George Alexander Forsyth was to raise a unit comprised of frontiersmen to conduct war against the hostiles. These frontiersmen, many of them combat veterans of the Civil War, were quartermaster employees and were recruited from Forts Hays and Harker. Considered scouts, each man had a Spencer repeating rifle and an army Colt revolver. All were expert shots, and apparently, this was a requirement to serve in the unit.[4] Major Forsyth's executive officer was Lieutenant Frederick H. Beecher (a nephew of the renowned Congregationalist, Henry Ward Beecher), and together, with these scouts, the men were determined to strike a blow against the Sioux and Cheyenne. Forsyth, summing up the mission of the modest band of warriors, said the following: "I had determined to find and attack the Indians, no matter what the odds might be against us. If we could not defeat them, we could show them that the government did not propose that they should escape unpunished for want of energy in their pursuit. I thought that with 51 men, even if I could not defeat them, they could not annihilate us. Furthermore, it was expected that the command would fight the Indians, and I meant it should do so."[5] Forsyth would get his chance soon enough.

Departing Fort Hays on August 29, 1868, Sheridan's best hope of retribution arrived at Fort Wallace on September 5. By this time, Wallace had become the jumping-off point into the land of Indian depredations. This area had remained a very dangerous place since Custer's arrival a year earlier. Soon after Forsyth's arrival, they received word about Indian attacks against a wagon train and the killing of several men. Forsyth and his men began the chase.

Reaching Sheridan, Kansas, in the western part of the state, Forsyth found a trail. It wasn't a large one, but as they followed it, it continued to grow and widen. Indeed, it became so wide that some of the scouts became a bit nervous as they realized confronting such a large number of Indians could be quite dangerous.[6] Sigmund Schlesinger, who would survive the ordeal, wrote about his experience as a member of Forsyth's strike force: "For several days we had been following an Indian trail so broad that it looked like a wagon-road. . . . Evidently they knew we were behind them, and seemed to be in a hurry to get away."[7] At one point they nearly caught up with the Indians, who, in their quick departure, had left behind numerous items such as cooking utensils, lodge poles, even the food that was being prepared. Although the command was running short of supplies, they refused to eat the "fresh antelope meat, quarters, etc."[8] This was no doubt an order directly from Major Forsyth, but one has to wonder how well this was received by the company at large.

By September 16, the command was camped along the north fork of the Arikaree River, in reality, a north fork of the Republican River. Unknown to Forsyth, he had camped only twelve miles downstream from two Indian villages. The sense that something was coming the next day pervaded the command, and they were correct. The Indians, under the leadership of Roman Nose of the Cheyenne, were making preparations to attack at dawn on September 17. Roman Nose fully expected to overwhelm the little band of scouts and accomplish his goal very quickly. What he didn't expect was being killed the next day.

At dawn, the Indians made good on their word. Forsyth, standing near one of the sentries, saw a feathered head, and as quickly as possible he aimed and fired, killing the young warrior. Immediately, the remainder of the Indians began yelling and waving blankets at the herd, hoping to create a stampede, but were quickly driven off. Once the first rifle shot had echoed throughout the camp, all hands grabbed their Spencer repeaters and prepared to defend themselves. Within moments, just as the dawn sky brought light to the men, Indians could be seen in all directions except the way the command had entered the area the day before.

Forsyth, believing this was a trick to draw them out of their cover, ordered his men to grab their horses and dash across the dry riverbed to the little sand island in the middle of the river. A second order was immediately given to dig rifle pits. Major Forsyth wasn't about to lose his men in some type of suicidal gauntlet, as if they were wild game. By 10:30 a.m., the warriors had launched a full-fledged assault on the position, but with the amount of firepower coming at them (seven rounds per man before having to reload), they took a number of casualties and were immediately repulsed. As there was no cover for the horses and mules, they began dropping or staggering around from their wounds.

Schlesinger remembers a pack mule wandering up to him with several arrows sticking out of him, and no doubt bullet wounds as well. Being in this shape, the scout remembered, ". . . caused him to rear and pitch to such an extent that Jim Lane, my neighbor, and I, decided to kill him. After shooting him he fell and lay between us, and served us the double purpose of food and barricade."[9] Soon there would be horse and mule meat and barricades for all.

After being sent reeling by Forsyth's defensive fire and two additional charges resulting in no ground gained by the Indians, the warriors chose to besiege the scouts, picking them off one by one through sniper fire, and this is what the scouts faced on the second day. On the third day they would conduct one final charge on the command, but it was halfhearted, and like the rest, soon aborted. The Indians, having at least succeeded in encircling the men, poured bullets in from all sides. The warriors also had the tactical advantage of firing from a slightly higher position, as the banks of the river were higher than the tiny island. As can be expected, casualties on this strip of sand continued to rise. Records of the fight reveal that on the second day of the siege, surgeon Dr. John H. Mooers was hit in the forehead by a bullet and died three days later. Lieutenant Frederick Beecher, a fine soldier and Civil War veteran who had distinguished himself during the 1863 battle of Gettysburg, was shot in the side. Instinctively knowing it was a death wound, he managed to crawl over to Major Forsyth and inform him.

Forever after, this tiny bit of land, so sacred to those who fought here, would be known as Beecher's Island.

Having lost all his horses, Forsyth dispatched two men under the cover of darkness to make the eighty-five-mile journey to Fort Wallace. It must have felt like a death sentence, leaving what little bit of safety the island had to offer on a trek that appeared impossible. Yet both men made it, and as the Indians withdrew on September 22, the only element left threatening the command was starvation. Having consumed the horses, the fighters had nothing left to eat, so it was a great relief when troopers of the Tenth Cavalry, the famous black regiment known as the Buffalo Soldiers, arrived on September 25 with food and extra mounts.

The prairie was still aflame with violence, just as it had been when George Custer had left it. He was needed again. He was vindicated. And best of all, he would return to the West with a job to do, absolutely confident of success. The tide would turn for Custer now, and he would soon put to rest the misgivings of any who had doubted his ability to win in all things. But surprises awaited him, and the Indians had confidence of their own.

Philip Sheridan had a plan. Frustrated by the army's inability to gain the upper hand in their fight against the Indians, he devised a strategy to strike them in a way they least expected. He wanted and truly believed that the element of surprise would work in their favor, and knew that he had to have the best troops possible to handle what needed to be done. He wanted a winter war, and he would use George Custer and the Seventh Cavalry to land a blow on their unsuspecting foes, so that all the Plains Indians would think twice about conducting war with the United States. Sheridan would receive only a portion of what he wanted, for just as Custer would strike that blow, the reverberations from his attack would be heard and felt for many years to come.

The camp Custer would ultimately attack was Black Kettle's, situated along the Washita River. Black Kettle, truly as much of an advocate for peace as the whites could hope for, nevertheless could not control every young brave who wanted to make war not just on white settlers, but on other Indians as well. No matter his intentions, this would not bode well for his safety or the safety of his people. Black Kettle, who managed to escape the hail of bullets at Sand Creek, would meet his second nightmare in the form of George Custer. This time, however, Black Kettle and his wife would not be as lucky, and the two would fall under the hail of pistol and rifle fire unleashed by the Seventh Cavalry. Oddly, Custer's attack upon Black Kettle's village occurred almost four years to the day after Sand Creek.

Custer began his trek into the wilderness on November 23, 1868. During the previous night the weather, as if allied with the Indians, dropped over a foot of snow on the command. Some of the troopers were no doubt dreading their march into this winter wonderland, but not Custer. He was certain the snow would work in their favor, greatly reducing the possibility of a move on the part of the Indians. Even Sheridan was calmed by Custer's confidence.

The Nineteenth Kansas Volunteer Cavalry, commanded by former Kansas governor Samuel J. Crawford, was to accompany Custer on this historic campaign, but was thwarted by the heavy snow. Having departed Topeka on November 5, the troops were destined to endure a brutal ordeal. Though spared the danger of Indian warfare, Crawford would nevertheless have his hands full battling the elements. Not until November 27—the day before the battle along the Washita would occur—would the weary and frozen Nineteenth Kansas enter base supply.

While the Nineteenth Kansas struggled, Custer was having his own problems. Not only was the deep snow straining both man and beast, whatever trail that may have been left by a recent war party was now under eighteen inches of snow. Already blanketing the prairie, the snow continued to fall, and at some point early in the march, the Osage scouts were unable to direct the command due to the blinding conditions. Even terrain ordinarily familiar to them was unrecognizable in this maze of white. Not to be deterred, Custer led the command himself with the use of a compass. On November 25, having had no luck on their chosen course, Custer changed direction and headed toward the Antelope Hills, reaching the Canadian Valley by nightfall.

Early the following morning, Major Elliott, with companies G, H, and M, rode off in search of telltale signs made by any war parties who, if still out, must surely be heading back to their winter camps. Meanwhile, the rest of the command was kept busy getting across the icy Canadian River. Thanks to the old scout, California Joe, they were able to find a suitable place for the troops to ford the river, a crossing which only took three hours. As Custer was about to start the regiment moving again, he spied a rider far off in the distance, plodding as fast as possible on the snow-encrusted plain. Soon the rider came into focus. It was none other than the scout Jack Corbin, bringing news from the now-distant Elliott. Custer's mind danced with imagination. What could Elliott have found? Had he located a trail, as Custer so desperately wanted? Or had he come up empty-handed and dispatched Corbin back to the main command for further orders? One can easily imagine the adrenaline rush Custer must have experienced as Corbin approached with what he hoped was good news, and the promise of an upcoming battle.

Corbin reined in his horse in front of Custer and gave him the news he most wanted to hear: Major Elliott had indeed discovered the trail of a war party numbering between 100 and 150 braves. Elated, Custer asked Corbin if he thought he could overtake Elliott if provided with a fresh mount. Corbin acknowledged that he could indeed, and soon the lone scout rode off into the blinding whiteness stretched out before him. Corbin had orders for the major that he was to continue the chase, but that if Custer had not caught up with him by nightfall, he was to stop and wait until the command could be joined. Custer realized that to have any real chance of catching Elliott, he would have to cut himself loose from the burdensome, slow-moving wagons. This he did, leaving eighty troopers to guard them under the command of the officer of the day, with orders to join the command as quickly as possible.

On this day, the officer of the day was Captain Louis McLane Hamilton. Young Hamilton, a grandson of the famous American Alexander Hamilton, was only twenty-three years old as he made this march to the Washita on a cold November day. That he was about to be left behind while his own company charged into battle did not sit well with the brave captain. Desiring to extricate himself from what he perceived as an unfortunate situation, Hamilton sought out Custer in hopes that he would change the order. While sympathizing with him, Custer was not about to force this duty on anyone else, although he did agree that should Hamilton find a replacement on his own, he would be allowed to accompany the main command into battle. Hamilton, who was very persistent in his search, convinced Second Lieutenant Edward Mathey, who was suffering from snow blindness, to remain behind as officer of the day. Unknown to young Hamilton, his fate was now sealed. If it were not for this unbelievable (in Hamilton's mind) stroke of luck, he might also have lived to become a grandfather. But all of this had changed, and Louis McLane Hamilton was now in the last hours of his life.

By 9:00 p.m., Custer was finally able to reach Major Elliott, who, like Hamilton, was also in the last hours of his life as well. Elliott had made camp near a stream adjacent to a timbered valley. The stream had deep banks which allowed the troops to build fires for making coffee, but still remain out of sight. However, this much-needed rest for man and beast would be short-lived. By 10:00 p.m.—and without the customary bugle calls—the regiment was again on the move. The Indian scouts had assured Custer that the camp of the enemy could not be far away.

Leading the column on foot three or four hundred yards in advance were the two Osage scouts, whose natural skill and ability obviously fascinated Custer. Later on he would write: ". . . they were our guides and the Panther, creeping upon its prey could not have advanced more cautiously or quietly than did these friendly Indians." Making reference to the strange, almost supernatural quality of their movements, he added: "They seemed to glide rather than walk over the snow-clad surface."[10] Behind the two dismounted scouts rode Custer with the other Osage and white scouts. The rest of the command rode four abreast, sometimes as far back as a half-mile. Custer wanted this distance to minimize the chance of the Indians being alerted to their presence by the sound of hundreds of horses' hooves crunching through the snow. Strict orders had been given that no communication was to be above a whisper, and those given to using tobacco had been forbidden from indulging themselves on this raw, cold evening. Custer was determined that the command remain undetected during this hunt.

Soon their nocturnal trek would be halted when the two Osage scouts stopped. When Custer rode up to ask what was the matter, one of the scouts responded in broken English, "Me don't know, but me smell fire."[11] Just then, several officers came out of the darkness to hear what the Indians had to say. As there was no white nose in the group that could perceive anything close to the smell of a fire, they concluded the Osage was mistaken. In minutes the column was again on the move, but after traveling only one mile the Osage again stopped and Custer was summoned for a second time. "Me told you so,"[12] the Osage whispered, pointing out the dying embers of a small fire. After a quick investigation, it was determined that it must have been used by those watching over the pony herds earlier.

Custer dismounted and followed one of the guides to the crest of a hill. While he stared out into the cold, dark night, he saw what appeared to be a mass of animals, but he couldn't be certain. The guide whispered to Custer that he heard the barking of a dog, which meant they were most likely near the village. Soon another dog was heard barking, and after that, the tinkling of a bell, which was good news, as the Indians often placed a bell around the neck of their lead pony. Custer, now convinced that his prey lay just before them, was already retracing his steps from the crest of the hill when he heard the wail of a child piercing the cold night air, coming from the valley below them. While this cry of an innocent did not deter him from his plan to attack the village, he did acknowledge regret "that in a war such as we were forced to engage in, the mode and circumstance of battle would possibly prevent discrimination."[13]

Now certain, Custer hurriedly assembled the officers. After having them quietly stack their sabers—he did not want any unnecessary clanging of metal—he took them to the crest of the hill. Unknown to the sleeping Cheyenne village, their enemy was now watching them and preparing to strike. Recalling the scene years later, Colonel Albert Barnitz said: "We all crept very quietly and slowly to the top of the ridge . . . and I could not help thinking that we very much resembled a pack of wolves."[14] After returning to where they had stacked their sabers, Custer informed them of his intentions to completely surround the village before the attack. After splitting his regiment into four detachments, Custer used the remaining hours of darkness to get his troops into position. Because of the distances they would have to cover just to get into position, two detachments left immediately, while a third began its role in the encirclement one hour before dawn. The morning air was extremely cold, and Custer had ordered that no fires were to be made; neither could anyone stamp their feet in an effort to keep warm. While the Cheyenne slept soundly, the blue-coated hunters readied themselves for war. On this night, the inexhaustible George Armstrong Custer would barely sleep one hour.

Before morning a strange apparition appeared that left Custer certain the enemy had discovered them and were even now raising a signal of alarm. However, what had appeared to be a bright rocket rising slowly above the doomed village was nothing but the brilliance of a morning star. Custer said it displayed "the most beautiful combination of prismatic tints," adding that it would remain a topic of conversation among Seventh Cavalry officers for many years to come.[15]

As daylight broke in the east, Custer gave the order to advance. Although the troopers were already suffering from the bitter cold, he ordered that haversacks and overcoats be removed so as not to encumber the men during battle. This was no doubt met with a variety of internal curses as the men laid their overcoats and equipment on the snowy ground.

The regiment was now completely separated, and Custer earnestly hoped that everyone was in place now that they were ready to begin their attack. Besides the mounted troops, Custer had wisely chosen forty sharpshooters under the command of Lieutenant W. W. Cooke. These men, who had a good field of fire from the trees along the river's edge, would be able to unleash a steady hail of lead against the warriors as they emerged from their tepees. Psychologically, this would be quite disturbing to the

Indians, as destruction would be coming not just from the mounted troopers but also from the dismounted and roving sharpshooters. This combined attack would have a devastating effect on the overwhelmed camp.

Custer led the column as the troops descended the long slope to the river. Directly across lay the sleepy Cheyenne encampment. Captain Louis Hamilton, who had fought so hard to accompany the regiment, was overheard encouraging his men to "keep cool and fire low." Heads bobbing, pistols in hand, the men soon had their first good glimpse of the white tepees of the still-undisturbed village. Just as Custer was about to give the signal for the band to begin playing the musical battle cry of the Seventh Cavalry, "Garryowen," the sound of a single rifle shot from the opposite end of the camp erupted in the morning air. The attack was on! Custer waved his hand, and for a few seconds the sound of "Garryowen" filled the valley floor, but again the elements would reign supreme, instantly freezing the men's saliva and rendering the instruments useless. What could not be silenced, however, were the cheers and the shouts of the men now sweeping down on the camp from all sides.

Unbeknownst to Custer, the rifle shot had come from an Indian "wrapped in a red blanket" who had discovered the troopers as he was guarding a herd of ponies and mules. This startled Cheyenne wasted no time in getting back into camp to warn the others. His rifle shot had roused many from sleep, and these men were already grabbing their weapons. Even so, the camp would quickly fall to Custer's four-pronged attack.

Charging down on the camp with Custer were companies A, D, K, and C, while Cooke and his sharpshooters were fanned out to the general's left, toward the tree-lined river's edge. Major Elliott, with companies G, H, and M, struck the village to the left of Custer, while Captain Edward Meyers, with companies E and I, attacked on Custer's right. Captain Thompson, with companies B and F, hit the camp almost directly in the rear, as did Lieutenant Godfrey with Troop K, whose orders were to rush through the village and seize the invaluable pony herd.

As always, Custer was at the head of his men as they rushed down the slope. It is unknown what thoughts may have been coursing through his mind at this time, but it is certain he was taking special pleasure in the battle—not just from having caught the Indians napping, but because he was back in the midst of warfare again, however brief the experience might be. And yet, he didn't have the luxury of contemplating the situation at hand, as the killing was about to begin. Quickly clearing the Washita River, Custer encountered a warrior clutching a rifle in his hand and immediately sent a bullet into his head. After running another brave down with his horse, Custer took up a position on a slight hill where he could oversee the fighting, giving orders as needed.

Captain Louis Hamilton, who was so happy to accompany the regiment, was charging the camp alongside Custer when a single rifle bullet split the side of his coat, killing him instantly. Those who witnessed the hit said he reeled in the saddle and fell dead. In an article published by the *New York Herald* on December 24, 1868, De Benneville Randolph Keim (a reporter accompanying the expedition) had this to say: "It was as the centre column was charging down the precipitous bluffs to cross the river and take the village that Captain Hamilton was killed. When struck he gave one convulsive start, stiffened in his stirrups, and was thus carried a corpse for a distance of several yards, when he fell from his horse." Several sources credit the Indian known as Cranky Man as the one who fired the fatal shot at Hamilton.

When Captain Frederick W. Benteen came charging into the pandemonium that was now Black Kettle's camp, he encountered an Indian boy that he suspected was not more than fourteen years old. Not regarding him as a warrior, Benteen began making hand signals indicating that the boy should surrender, but the youth had other ideas. As Benteen held his fire, the young Cheyenne sent a bullet past the captain's head. At this point, almost any other member of the Seventh Cavalry would have gladly killed the boy, and would have been correct in doing so, but not the coolheaded Captain Benteen, who continued to hold his fire. Two more shots were fired, the second of which struck Benteen's horse in the neck, hurling him into the snow. Enough was enough. Benteen's pistol cracked and the boy fell dead. The lifeless form lying before Benteen was Blue

Horse, a nephew of Black Kettle. That Benteen allowed his opponent to shoot three times before firing the fatal shot revealed his sincere desire to spare the boy's life. Even so, it would remain a source of regret to the captain for many years.

Throughout the camp the disorganized sounds of battle filled the air: the shouts of the war cry, the pitiful screams of the children who could not fathom why such violence had come to their village, and the unmistakable wail of the wounded which can follow a direct hit. A young girl by the name of Moving Behind, who was only fourteen years old at the time of the battle, recalled years later just how difficult it was for anyone to escape from the heavy firing of Custer's troops: "The air was full of smoke from gunfire . . . we could see the red fire of the shots."[16] The entire valley must have been filled with the smell of burnt gunpowder. While concealing herself as best as possible, Moving Behind could easily hear the groaning of the wounded ponies that sounded almost human to her ears.

Attacking with Benteen's column was Colonel Albert Barnitz. Although an able soldier, Barnitz did not share Benteen's sympathy for the Indians, although the two men shared a mutual dislike for Custer. In any event, Barnitz recalled how his troops came face-to-face with a group of Cheyenne fleeing the opposite end of the camp, and how a number of these were immediately killed, while the remainder was driven to a nearby ravine where they were soon cut down. When Barnitz and Major Elliott spotted another group running toward the pony herds, the order was given to fire. But when none of the Cheyenne were seen to drop, Sergeant McDermott and some men were ordered to give chase. When Barnitz caught up with these Indians he discovered that they were only women and children, and, "not caring to waste ammunition on them," decided to hold his fire.[17]

Barnitz would find himself in a type of duel with an Indian just minutes later. Having tried numerous times but failing to properly position himself to unleash a good shot on the warrior, shots rang out from both parties at almost the same time, and at point-blank range. Although Barnitz's pistol had found its mark, so had the Indian's old Lancaster rifle, the shot so close that it left a burn mark on his coat. Unknown to Barnitz, the bullet had entered his left side and exited his right side without doing any significant, long-lasting damage, yet when doctors Lippincott and Renick examined him, they declared the wound to be fatal. Even Custer, who had seen hundreds of men expire in battle, felt that he had but minutes to live, writing, "[H]is face wore that pale deathly aspect so common and peculiar to those mortally wounded."[18] When Dr. Lippincott dispatched Lieutenant Godfrey to carry the message to Barnitz that his recovery was in doubt, Barnitz, feeling far more optimistic, blurted out: "Oh Hell! They think because my extremities are cold I am going to die, but if I could get warm I'm sure I'll be alright."[19] Barnitz was right; death would not come to him for many years.

For the most part, the Cheyenne were quickly overwhelmed, either shot and killed, wounded, or gathered up as prisoners. Although for the first few minutes of the attack it appeared the camp was in utter pandemonium, the momentum of the battle was clearly in Custer's favor due to the element of surprise. However, some Indians had managed to take up positions of cover, and these warriors were determined to fight it out. At one point, the scout Ben Clark, who had ridden beside Custer into the camp, informed him about some troops belonging to Meyer's company that were chasing and firing into a group of fleeing women and children. Clark asked Custer if he wanted those people killed. Custer, undoubtedly a warrior but not a murderer, said no, and then added, "Ride out there and give the officer commanding my compliments and ask him to stop it."[20] Those not already killed were gathered up as prisoners.

Soon, however, other warriors were seen near the village. They had come from the nearby Sioux and Arapaho camps situated along the Washita, farther downstream. Indeed, for a stretch of about fifteen miles along the Washita River (in present-day Oklahoma), which the Indians called Lodgepole River,[21] the Cheyenne, Arapaho, Kiowa, Sioux, Comanche, and Kiowa-Apache (a total of about six thousand Indians), were in their winter camps.[22] The battle Custer was even then conducting was drawing warriors like a magnet from the nearest of these camps due to the heavy firing of their weapons. Add to this those Indians lucky enough to escape the slaughter and join their brothers downstream and you had a recipe for disaster for the Seventh Cavalry, if the Indians had been able to mount a coordinated attack quickly enough. For their part, the Indians—even those like Black Kettle, who wanted peace but realized that the young braves in his camp could not be controlled and might provoke the wrath of the whites—did not expect the army to attack them in a winter campaign. They were wrong. But now that the fight was on, the warriors downriver were grabbing their rifles and other weapons and hurrying toward the battle. And because the ebb and flow of battle is so unpredictable, no matter which side has the upper hand, an event was about to occur in Custer's regiment that was completely unexpected, given the unbelievable success they were having in conquering Black Kettle's camp.

When Major Elliott spotted a group of Indians making their escape, he decided to give chase with nineteen of his men. Benteen would later describe Elliott's adventure as "going off on his own hook." Indeed, Lieutenant Hale overheard Elliott shout out, "Here goes for a brevet or a coffin" just as the men put spurs to their horses and galloped away. But there would be no promotion for the major at the end of this ride. Unfortunately for Elliott, he and his doomed troopers would run directly into a large group of warriors coming to the Cheyenne camp's rescue. Whatever damage the soldiers were able to inflict on this band must have been minimal, and very quickly, all were killed and subsequently mutilated.

Custer, completely unaware of the number of villages in the area, or how close they were to each other, was soon informed by Lieutenant Godfrey that while his company was gathering up the pony herds, he had taken some time to scout the land east of the village. Here he found an even larger body of warriors than the ones previously spotted by the command, and unbeknownst to them, it was a larger band than the one which had destroyed Elliott's tiny command. When the general first heard Godfrey's report, he exclaimed: "What's that?," but as the lieutenant explained, it became very clear to Custer: After Godfrey had spied the mass of dismounted Indians running down the opposite end of the valley, he had quickly turned over the captured ponies to Lieutenant Law and given chase. Obviously, Godfrey was being driven by the same type of fatal thinking which had taken Major Elliott to his death. In any event, the platoon pressed onward.

After clearing the stream, Godfrey followed the Indians' trail, locating them, now mounted, in a wooded draw where a larger pony herd had been concealed. The inquisitive lieutenant continued to follow the trail on the hills rising above the valley, and as he did so, he passed a lone tepee. Just beyond this he spotted two mounted Indians, riding in a circle. "I knew the circling of the warriors meant an alarm and rally. But I wanted to see what was in the valley beyond them."[23] Godfrey's unbridled rashness was soon tempered by the warnings of two veteran sergeants, Conrad and Hughes, concerning the real dangers of continuing on. Leaving the rest of the men, Godfrey climbed a nearby ridge to obtain a better view. "I was amazed," Godfrey would write, "to find that as far as I could see . . . there were tepees—tepees."[24] Not only that, but as was the case with Major Elliott, warriors were coming to meet them. Godfrey's troops were then forced to fight a retreating action all the way to Black Kettle's conquered village. Luckily, they would suffer no casualties in their hurried withdrawal.

As the hills surrounding the village began to sprout warriors, it appears the immensity of what could be out there began to play on Custer's mind. As time was of the essence, Custer now turned his attention to reducing the camp to rubble. Tepees, buffalo robes, and anything combustible was now torched. Custer would, however, carry away and later present to a Michigan historical society an ornate Cheyenne shield, and the scalp of the warrior who carried it (because rules did not apply to him in the same way they did to others). The ponies which Custer had ordered gathered up numbered around eight or nine hundred. After culling out about two hundred of these to transport women, children, and prisoners, Custer ordered the rest shot.

Without question, the "battle" of the Washita added a new dimension to Custer's life. No longer was he just a Civil War icon; now he was well on his way to becoming a real-life Indian fighter. He had engulfed Black Kettle's camp and destroyed it, and he had done so under the most arduous of weather conditions. It was a triumph for this lover of all things war. But there was a black spot right in the middle of his victory, and it would never go away. Indeed, it would cause a rift in the Seventh Cavalry that would never heal. That black spot was the mystery surrounding the disappearance of Major Elliott and his nineteen men. Thus far the Seventh had sustained only one death—Louis Hamilton—and while the loss was total for the deceased lieutenant, it was a casualty figure unheard of for a battle of this size, with the wounded numbering as few as sixteen.

But as the snowy hills and valleys around them began to fill with young warriors, Custer considered the possibilities of a combined attack overwhelming his coveted command. In his writings later on, he would supposedly convey his true feelings in the matter, but given the situation which had, in fact, occurred, it is far more likely that he became somewhat unnerved with the number of Indians dancing in his head, and mentally cut loose Elliott and his command—a command he probably believed (quite correctly) had already been overtaken and killed. Of course, this was not the soldierly thing to do, and he'd received criticism from many directions, including General Sheridan, for he owed it to Elliott and the men to render aid if needed, or to at least discover what had happened to them. Instead, Custer made haste getting out of the wilderness.

On December 10, the Seventh Cavalry was camped along the Washita, some six miles from the ruins of Black Kettle's camp. This time, General Sheridan was accompanying Custer to see for himself the site of the battle. They set out early the next morning, and in less than two hours arrived at the destroyed village. Soon search parties were sent out to discover the fate of Major Elliott and his men. After Custer and Sheridan rode to a nearby ridge, the boy general explained to his commander the lay of the land and how the battle had unfolded. After a while, the search parties fanned out in different directions. Custer, Sheridan, Keim (the New York reporter), and a number of troopers started to search, following the trail down the Washita in the direction the missing men were known to have traveled.[25] Unbelievably, within a hundred yards, the first mutilated body was found, and another hundred yards brought them to an open field where Elliott and the rest of his men were sprawled. All had been killed fighting for their lives, and all had been horribly mutilated. It was not an unexpected find, but sobering nevertheless.

It's anybody's guess what Custer was thinking at this moment, and it's not found in any of his writings. For many who were there, and for those who would hear of the events along the Washita, there was a real sense that Custer had abandoned Elliott and his troops to their fate. It would be a turning point for the Seventh Cavalry, dividing the group into those who felt Custer was the villain in the matter, and those who believed leaving the field of battle without knowing what happened to them was the correct thing to do.

Also found later that day, farther downstream at another abandoned camp, were the bodies of Clara Blinn, twenty-one, and her two-year-old son, Willie. The two had been captured from a wagon train on October 7. The skull of the child had been crushed, and Clara had suffered two bullet wounds to the head. They were no doubt being held at the camp where their bodies were recovered and had apparently been murdered during Custer's attack of Black Kettle's camp.

By the time the command returned to Fort Cobb in late December, Captain Frederick Benteen was livid about Custer's refusal to search for Elliott and his men. Never one to not speak his mind and always willing to record his thoughts in ink, Benteen wrote a detailed letter to a friend describing the events which had occurred along the Washita, ripping Custer apart in the process. Unbeknownst to Benteen, his friend sent a copy of the letter to the *St. Louis Democrat,* which gladly published it, and it was almost immediately picked up by the *New York Times.* Benteen's friend, not wishing to cause the captain any trouble with his superiors, sent the letter without a signature. When Custer learned of the letter, he was hopping mad. The letter contained details of the campaign that only one who had been present during the battle would have known. The thought that anyone under his command would write such a thing was past understanding, and here the boy in Custer would cause the man to act rashly once again.

Casting aside military procedure, Custer gathered his officers together in his tent, and like an enraged schoolmaster who'd been pressed a little too far by his students, he was determined to exact some physical distress from the author of this latest betrayal. There he was, walking back and forth with a riding crop in his hand (the tool of punishment, one must assume), all the while breathing out threats of a whipping to the writer or writers of this treacherous slap in the face. It was drama at its best, but it was about to backfire in a most humiliating way for Custer, who, in all probability, did not expect to have to actually confront the one responsible. After all, who would be foolish enough to admit such an insubordination as this? He obviously didn't consider Benteen.

As Custer unleashed the verbal diatribe, Benteen listened calmly just inside the doorway of the tent. Benteen, who, like Custer, never seemed to exhibit fear, was not about to be castigated by anyone in the matter and decided to give the boy general just what he wanted. Stepping outside of the tent just long enough to check his army revolver, making sure it was in proper working order, he moved back inside and waited for the proper pause in Custer's threats before blurting out: "General Custer, while I cannot father all of the blame you have asserted, still, I guess I am the man you are after, and I am ready for the whipping promised."[26] At this, Custer began to stammer (a common occurrence whenever he became excited), and could only respond: "Colonel Benteen, I'll see you again, sir."[27] Benteen had made Custer the fool in this encounter. Custer had started it, but the captain had finished it. It wasn't just about words or making Custer look foolish. There was a definite finality to what Benteen was doing, for as angry as Custer was, there is every reason to believe that Benteen expected Custer to make good on his promise of assaulting the writer of the scandalous letter. As Benteen alluded to years later, "[H]ad the rawhide whirred," as he put it, the confrontation certainly would have turned deadly. Of course, killing Custer does appear extreme. Still, there is no reason to doubt Benteen's claim of instant and fatal retribution for

Custer had he delivered the promised whipping. Benteen would have killed Custer on the spot, and every officer present would have testified as to what Custer had done to bring about his unfortunate demise. In the end, however, Custer backed down.

This was a pivotal time in Custer's life. He'd established himself as an Indian fighter and would forever be connected with a difficult march, the destruction of a large Indian village, and his ability to get the kind of results the top brass of the army was looking for. It would, however, come with a price, for unlike the unifying battles of the Civil War, his victory along the Washita that cold and snowy November of 1868 would create a schism within the Seventh Cavalry that would never be healed.

There is an interesting footnote to the Washita battle. In March of 1869, Custer was seeking the release of two white women who were being held captive by the Cheyenne. The struggle between whites and Indians had not abated, and although Custer had Indian captives of his own, he was determined to secure their release unharmed. While there probably wasn't a Cheyenne alive who didn't want Custer dead, he arranged for a parley to save the women's lives. As Custer, Lieutenant W. W. Cooke, and Mo-nah-se-tah, a beautiful young Indian woman acting as Custer's interpreter, entered the Cheyenne village, it would be Mo-nah-se-tah who would confirm the women's presence.[28] As Custer and Cooke sat down in the chief's lodge, Custer was placed beneath the medicine arrows (a very sacred symbol to the Cheyenne) and was soon sharing in the Indian custom of smoking the peace pipe. Also participating in the ceremony was the medicine man, who, unknown to Custer, was spewing out Cheyenne promises of destruction should Custer ever again use violence against their people. The medicine man then proceeded to pour the ashes from the pipe bowl onto the same boots which had conquered Black Kettle's Washita camp, the intent of which was to bring bad luck on this continually lucky officer. Only time would tell.

A brief mention of Mo-nah-se-tah: Although no photograph exists of this woman, from all accounts she was very beautiful, possessing the finest facial features, and must have been a real head-turner. Certainly, she stood out from many of the others, and obviously impressed Custer from the moment he first saw her as they gathered up prisoners during the attack on Black Kettle's camp. At this time she was seven months pregnant, and her father, Chief Little Rock, had been killed in the battle. Writing about her, Custer said she "was an exceedingly comely squaw, possessing a bright, cheery face, a countenance beaming with intelligence, and a disposition more inclined to be merry than one usually finds among Indians."[29] Custer also noticed her "bright laughing eyes, a set of pearly teeth [Libbie referred to them as being white, straight teeth], a rich complexion, her well-shaped head was crowned with a luxuriant growth of the most beautiful silken tresses, rivaling in color the blackness of the Raven and extending, when allowed to fall loosely over her shoulders, to below her waist."[30]

Nothing has been passed down to us through the record that would absolutely connect Custer sexually with this beautiful young woman. That said, it does seem likely they were in fact together for a while, and the rumor exists both in the white and Indian cultures that she bore him a child. It also appears that his relationship with Mo-nah-se-tah was a bone of contention with Libbie, as she may have had her suspicions. In any event, the relationship was of short duration.

CHAPTER 8

A Calm before the Storm

In April 1871, the Seventh Cavalry was sent to Kentucky, setting up headquarters in Louisville. Apparently this border state—one that had managed to stay within the Union during the Civil War, but was still represented by one of the thirteen stars on the Confederate States flag anyway—was having trouble controlling some of its citizens who had taken up the cause of a new group known as the Ku Klux Klan. This, as well as the attempt by the federal government to stabilize those portions of the South that could be given to trouble, meant that two companies of this now-famous cavalry unit would be garrisoned at Elizabethtown, Kentucky, with the remaining companies scattered throughout the South where trouble was breaking out, or was anticipated. For Custer, however, who would not join up with the regiment until early September, it would be exceedingly light duty when compared to the rigors, deprivations, and dangers encountered on the Great Plains, and it would provide some much-needed rest before the regiment once again headed west, toward their march with destiny.

Custer would not arrive in Kentucky until September of 1871, and while he had kind things to say concerning the sleepy little town and its inhabitants, Libbie, who would soon join him, apparently never got over her dislike of the region. The Custers did, however, enjoy coming to Louisville, where an active social life was available to them. From grand balls held at the Galt House Hotel on Main Street, to evenings at the theater, to the purchasing of beautiful thoroughbreds in Louisville and Lexington, the couple obviously reveled in their notoriety and the attention they received. Custer even enjoyed a visit in 1872 with his buffalo-hunting partner from the Plains, the Grand Duke Alexis of Russia. Not only did they wine and dine the visiting royals in Louisville, but they also made a trip to Mammoth Cave on the duke's train.

Custer would also make use of this time stalking the plentiful game of the bluegrass country, and while it was not the same exciting romp as a several-mile run over the Great Plains, it did soothe his need for the hunt. And just as was their custom when they were stationed at Fort Hays, the Custers were often seen horseback riding together. Custer would also spend time writing and refining his articles for *Galaxy* magazine, detailing his part in the Hancock Expedition.[1]

Besides the cavalry contingent, an infantry company was also garrisoned in the town. All military personnel were housed in buildings located close to the town's square, and the people were daily witnesses to the structure and activities of the army. That being the case, it was well known by the locals that any immediate action needing to be taken by the troops as a whole would be proceeded by the sounding of a bugle, with the bugler playing the proper notes depending on the type of "emergency" being announced. As such, on occasion, some of "the local lads would contrive to break the monotony of this duty by sounding bugle calls at odd hours sending the troopers tumbling out of their billets into formation."[2]

Such an idyllic life could not last forever, nor would Custer be happy without the shouting and firing of a battle. He was meant for war, and no matter what other activities or people he found enjoyable in life, the call of conflict, the unknown activity of the enemy, the hunt to avenge the latest outrage on the Great Plains, would always take precedence over the daily, reserved living of the civilian. There had to be action to give his life meaning, and the nearly two years the Seventh Cavalry spent sequestered away in Kentucky, chasing invisible enemies, left him yearning for the real action that awaited him. Not only had nothing really changed on the prairie, but the problems with the unruly Indians had actually started to multiply with the discovery of gold in the Black Hills. Treaties signed by the United States government were being broken, and a flood of white humanity was now invading areas sacred to the Indians. This was a situation that was destined to end in slaughter.

———❦———

Although the government had had some success in permanently corralling many Indians onto the reservations, some, like the Sioux, were having no part of it. Indeed, even reservation Indians would often depart in the warmer months to run free with their people on the Plains. These were referred to as *summer roamers*. *Winter roamers* were Indians who refused all cooperation with the whites, including reservation life, and they did not take the food and supplies offered to those inhabiting the various reservations.[3] The Sioux reservation comprised most of South Dakota, and they were allowed to hunt in unceded territories, from northeastern Wyoming (which included the Black Hills) to southeastern Montana, including the Yellowstone River basin. This would prove to be a hotly contested region, as the Sioux did not like the white encroachment onto land they considered theirs, spearheaded by the Northern Pacific Railroad.

The Indians knew that the "Iron Horse" was the forerunner of the flood of white faces. Once the railroad began stretching across the Plains, white expansion would explode, more forts would line the horizon, and the military would be there to ensure that all went well. This was the case in Kansas and Nebraska, and it would be so here. The sticking point with the Sioux, however, was that the unceded territory, where they were hunting and otherwise conducting their lives, was now being invaded, and even Sherman warned Sheridan in 1872: "That Northern Pacific Road is going to give you a great deal of trouble. . . . The Indians will be hostile in an extreme degree. . . ."[4] Sherman, of course, was hoping this expansion would finally bring a "final solution" to the Indian problem. The very choice of words speaks volumes as to his feelings about the matter, and it lends credence to those Indians who were resisting the whites at every turn. In truth, if the incursion brought about a full-fledged Indian war, this was fine with Sherman and many of the top brass, for the crushing of the Sioux was the eventual plan anyway. This "crushing" would be a long time coming, and there would be the decimation of many whites before the problem no longer existed.

Since Custer and his Seventh Cavalry had been chosen to be the instrument of correction for Sioux disobedience, they were assigned to the Department of the Dakotas, headquartered in St. Paul, Minnesota. The authority of the department stretched throughout the Dakotas, including all of Montana. The Teton Sioux, comprising six tribes—Oglala, Sans Arc, Blackfoot, Hunkpapa, Miniconjou, Brule—were a warrior people, and along with the Northern Cheyenne and a smattering of Northern Arapaho, would be the most difficult to subjugate. In the greater scheme of things, practically everyone on the continent, both Indian and white, understood the power being unleashed by the expansion of millions of Europeans in the West. Everyone knew this would result in the eventual defeat of the Plains Indians, but that didn't matter. Whatever gains were going to be made by the whites, the young warriors were going to see them pay a heavy price for it. General William Tecumseh Sherman, now a man of nearly fifty, understood this and cautioned that the road to victory would be costly. Yet neither he nor General Sheridan had any real grasp of how high that cost would be. While they understood that the direct incursion into Indian lands would lead to a strong backlash of revolt from the Sioux and Cheyenne, they were completely ignorant of the fact that they were actually setting the stage for disaster along the Little Bighorn, just a few years down the road. In their minds, such an egregious disaster was unthinkable. It was a devaluing of Indian fighting abilities, and it would cost them dearly.

When the command packed up and left Louisville, it was leaving the relative peace of the civilized world behind. Out on the Great Plains were the real dangers, and this was the only place left on the continent where Custer was likely to find war. Indeed, he craved the life the open prairie offered, and his thinking about the West was much like the thinking of those he hoped to subjugate. In these uncharted territories, life was as it had been for thousands of years. The game was plentiful, and every mile they galloped over revealed a vista Custer had never seen before. At the center of it all was the surety of battle with a people who were not going to relinquish territory without a fight. Where this might have troubled some who wore a military uniform, it was a welcome call for Custer.

When the command reached Yankton, Dakota Territory, they marched up the Missouri River to Fort Rice. It was an arduous journey of some four hundred miles, and for the newer troops who were not veterans of previous expeditions, it was an eye-opener. Of course, not everyone would be happy to see Custer, for his past actions—of which the "battle" along the Washita was only a part—had had a deep and lasting effect on many of the junior officers. These flaws of Custer's, so easily detected by those around him and known even by many of his supporters, were never considered by the boy general. Whatever decision Custer made at any moment of the day or night was considered by him to be the correct move. His presence for many was an irritant to be tolerated and avoided if at all possible. Where Custer failed in diplomatic relations, he made up for as a commander in the field. His ability to respond tactically in dangerous situations was a skill he had sharply honed, and it would without question save lives during the fighting with the Sioux. This alone should have made up for many of his shortcomings. Not even his future commander, General David S. Stanley, liked him. Having heard about Custer's petty ways and his often-cavalier attitude while leading his command, he expected to butt heads with him and soon learned firsthand the truth behind the rumors. Stanley, a Civil War veteran and winner of the Medal of Honor for his actions at the battle of Franklin, Tennessee, on November 30, 1864, had his own limitations. Like many who wore the uniform, he had an attachment to the bottle. This being the case, his stone-throwing carried only so much power.

What would be called the Yellowstone Expedition would commence in late June of 1873. It was an immense effort consisting of ten cavalry companies under Custer, and twenty companies of infantry, including two squadrons of artillery. The command also had 27 scouts and interpreters, as well as 353 civilians manning 275 wagons filled with food, munitions, and forage, the grand total being some 1,500 men. The strength of horses and mules stood at 2,321, according to army records. It was definitely a show of force that had teeth. As General Stanley's official report would later decree, it was an expedition "designed for the protection of engineering surveyors of the Northern Pacific Railroad."[5] Among the civilian contingent were six representatives from the Smithsonian Institution, whom the soldiers referred to as "bug hunters."[6] As always, Custer would be at the front of his troops and would often ride ahead with a small unit for hunting game or to scout the territory.

The Indians had enough manpower to strike the army and could field a war party of up to a thousand braves or greater, such was their strength on the Northern Plains. Whatever deficiencies they encountered while engaging such a large force, they always retained the ability to quickly break off an engagement and escape. So the Indians were not in the least intimidated by the army's presence; on the contrary, they were ready to strike back.

The expedition left Fort Rice on Friday, June 20, 1873. Wearing a bright red shirt made by Libbie, Custer was once again standing out from the crowd.[7] Almost from the start, the expedition encountered a heavy rain, and while there were periods of relief, it continued pouring for the better part of two weeks. This made progress slower than expected and created havoc for the horses maneuvering through the muddy trail and even more trouble for the heavy wagons. Despite the inclement weather, the expectation of a productive campaign was in the air. Private Charles Windolph, twenty-one, of Benteen's company H, had joined the Seventh Cavalry in 1870. He had grown weary "playing soldier" when the regiment was headquartered in Kentucky (he was stationed in Nashville), and he was looking forward to finally seeing some action after Custer was ordered to Dakota Territory. "It'd be fun," he immediately thought, "to do a little Indian fighting." Expressing his view of the mood of most of his fellow troopers, Windolph added: "All we knew or cared about was that we were going into the last of the real Indian country."[8] Windolph would not be disappointed.

It is both interesting and humorous to note that both General Stanley and Lieutenant Colonel Custer anticipated trouble with each other, and as men will do, they both wrote home to their wives about it. Stanley could not stand the fact that Custer was already riding ahead of the main command with a small contingent of troops, and as the column was attempting to cross Muddy River when it was swollen from the torrential rains, Custer was once again miles ahead, scouting. He had sent a rider back to Stanley asking for supplies and forage. Seizing the moment, Stanley sent back a terse message ordering him to stop the march and come and get what he needed himself. Writing to his wife, Stanley said: "I had a little flurry with Custer as I told you I probably would. We were separated 4 miles, and I intended him to assist getting the train, his own train, over the Muddy River. Without consulting me he marched off 15 miles, coolly sending me a note to send him forage and rations. I sent for him, ordered him to halt where he was, to unload his wagons, and send for his own rations and forage, and never to presume to make another move without orders."[9]

Such pettiness must have annoyed Custer. He wasn't dealing with Philip Sheridan, that was for sure. But Stanley was his commanding officer, so Custer returned with his men and oversaw the building of a pontoon bridge across the river. Stanley wasn't through with Custer yet. After ordering him to never launch ahead without direct orders from him, he positioned the cavalry at the rear of the column and placed his insubordinate cavalry commander under arrest. This was certainly petty, and if he wanted to get under Custer's skin by forbidding him to do the things he most enjoyed and saw as useful to the regiment, very effective. There was an unexpected bright spot at this time: Custer's old friend and Civil War adversary, General Thomas Rosser, was now chief engineer of surveyors for the Northern Pacific Railroad, and unbeknownst to Custer, Rosser had caught up with his old friend, having departed Fort Rice on June 23. As Custer was resting on a buffalo robe in his tent, he heard the unmistakable voice of Rosser inquiring where he might find Custer's tent. The two had not talked in many years, so the reunion was a happy one.

Soon Stanley would once again unleash Custer, allowing him to do what he did best. Custer's value as a commander, and his ability to think quickly under fire in battle, would come into play when their first real confrontation with the Sioux occurred on August 4. Taken directly from General Stanley's report, he "sent Lieut. Col. Custer ahead to look up the road, a service for which he always volunteered. About 2 p.m. I came up to one of my scouts, who told me there was firing ahead, but thought it was buffalos, as he had observed a trail of these animals going in that direction. Shortly two scouts and a cavalry straggler ran in and said they had been pursued by Indians."[10] Stanley immediately sent the remainder of the cavalry toward Custer.

Custer, who had scouted about ten miles ahead of the command, was the recipient of an old Indian ruse: Having camped with about ninety troops (two companies, including five officers) along a strip of land opposite the mouth of the Tongue River, in a stand of timber, the troops were resting around noon on this exceedingly hot day. One estimate put the temperature as high as 110 degrees. The horses, grazing nearby, were guarded by the pickets, the first line of defense should there be trouble. If any trouble was going to pop up, it would be met with the firing of army carbines and the yelling of "Indians!" Indeed, Bloody Knife, Custer's trusted scout, had warned the general that day that signs of Sioux activity in the area were plentiful and that an attack could most likely be expected. The site of the encounter is very near Miles City, Montana, in the south-eastern portion of the state.

As the men rested their backs on their saddles, catching up on some uncomfortable but much-needed sleep, six warriors came dashing across the plains from the west in an attempt to scatter the cavalry horses. The pickets, having sounded the alarm, brought the soldiers to their feet, a number of which quickly grabbed and cocked the hammers on their carbines. Within seconds, they sent a volley of lead toward the Sioux. Having scattered them momentarily, the Indians revealed their true purpose for their raid by not galloping away. They wanted the soldiers to pursue them, and Custer would oblige. The cavalrymen moved quickly, tossing saddles across their mounts and strapping them on. Taking his brother Tom, his orderly, his brother-in-law, James Calhoun, and twenty troopers, Custer dashed after the small party with the full knowledge it could be a trap. He ordered Myles Moylan to follow with the remainder of the troops. Custer was not about to let the Indians get away unchallenged.

After about a two-mile chase (the Indians would slow down when the soldiers slowed the pace of their horses), Custer, riding a fast Kentucky horse, decided to take his orderly, who also was well mounted, and put some distance between him and Tom Custer's troops. Although still believing that an ambush was in the works, Custer wanted to at least attempt to control the situation, and so, after galloping on another two hundred yards or so, he stopped (as did the Indians) and signaled Tom to halt his march. This accomplished, he began walking his horse in a circle, the traditional sign for a parley, but the six warriors guided their ponies to the cottonwood trees, to Custer's left. If one could have had a bird's-eye view at this time, one would have seen Custer and his orderly, followed a distance of some several hundred yards by Tom Custer's men, and farther still, Moylan's troops trotting far off in the distance.

The six Indians, now edging toward the cottonwood trees along the river, acted as if they were leaving the field, but this was only part of the ruse. As Custer watched them trot away, he sent his orderly back to tell Tom he should keep an eye on the bushes to his left, about three hundred yards away. The orderly galloped off, passed the message to Tom Custer, and had almost reached Custer on his return when all hell broke loose. "The orderly had delivered his message," Custer remembered, "and had almost rejoined me, when . . . the small party in front had faced toward us and were advancing as if to attack. I could scarcely credit the evidence of my eyes, but my astonishment had only begun when turning to the wood on my left I beheld bursting from their concealment between three and four hundred Sioux warriors. . . ."[11] When Custer saw the large body of Sioux emerge from the timber, he pulled hard on the reins of his horse, dug in his spurs, and began the race toward Tom and the men. The warriors, faces painted and heads adorned with feathers or wearing the full war bonnet, shouted the war cry as they galloped at full speed to reach the riders. They were hoping to intercept the two lone cavalrymen and kill them, thereby annihilating the duo before sweeping Tom Custer's tiny command.

As Custer raced back to the troops, he started yelling "Dismount your men! Dismount your men!" but Tom couldn't hear him. Within seconds, however, Tom Custer took control, gave the order to dismount, and prepared the men to fight on foot (every fourth man, however, remained on his horse and held the reins of the other three). Being outnumbered by as many as twenty to one, it would require all the skill and concealment the army could muster. There was a problem, though: There wasn't any cover or concealment available, so the men had to file out and make a skirmish line. Dropping down on one or both knees, they raised their carbines and took careful aim. As Custer and the orderly raced through the thin defensive line, the troops, many of them skilled in Indian warfare, gave the warriors a volley of lead which caused those in front to scatter. Two more quick blasts and the Indians understood that the soldiers, even exposed as they were, were putting out a volume of fire that was going to do serious damage to their assault. A number of warriors had already been hit, and now the Indians were retreating back into the woods. This would be fortunate for Custer, as it gave Myles Moylan additional time to reach the beleaguered command. Had the Indians pressed their attack despite the withering fire, the Sioux no doubt would have killed them all before help could come. The arrival of Moylan's troops was essential in Custer's survival.

Moylan and his men brought the troops together, but they were in the middle of the prairie, subject to attack from every direction. It was quickly determined they'd fare better if they got closer to the river, forming a defensive position there. The Indians, wasting no time, once again started pouring out of the woods. They would not make another combined frontal attack this time, but instead would attempt separate attacks by small groups, one of their favorite fighting styles. Custer would later record how the men stayed calm during this time, some even making jokes.

Forming a circular defensive line (the diameter of this irregular moving circle being several hundred yards) did offer the cavalrymen some protection, as the horses were kept in the middle, which meant that fire from the opposite side was likely to hit the mounts and perhaps their riders, who were still in the saddle. "As we were falling back," Custer wrote, "contesting each foot of ground passed over, I heard a sudden sharp cry of pain from one of the men in charge of our horses; the next moment I saw his arm hanging helplessly at his side, while a crimson current flowing near his shoulder told that the aim of the Indians had not been entirely in vain."[12]

Custer and his men finally made it to the timber line, and once the horses were safely shielded in the woods, he ordered every eighth man to hold the horses instead of the usual four. For the next several hours, as the troopers lay stretched out on the bank of a dry creek bed in a semicircle, they took careful aim and kept firing at those warriors boldly riding up close to the line or attempting to creep through the high prairie grass. At one point an Indian attempted to get farther downstream and lead a party of warriors to a spot where they could attack the soldiers from behind, but he was spotted and driven off. When this failed, the Indians tried torching the grass, hopeful of driving them to the river, but it wouldn't burn properly. Having lost the momentum early in the fight (and their only real chance of overwhelming the cavalrymen), the Sioux were soon at a loss as to what to do. During the fight, ammunition began to run low. Custer sent back some men to retrieve the spare ammo that was still on the horses, or belonging to the wounded, and this brought a welcome supply. Soon the fire Custer's men were taking became sporadic and then drifted out altogether. Scanning the bluffs above them, the hot and exhausted troops saw the unmistakable large plume of dust signaling the fast approach of a large body of troops. This sight, which guaranteed their survival, had been seen first by the Sioux, and was in fact the reason for their departure. Not willing to let any opportunity go, Custer ordered the men to mount, and along with the forces of General Stanley, gave chase to the fleeing Indians. They were never able to close with the Sioux, who were able to make their customary escape.

The Seventh Cavalry would suffer eleven dead and numerous wounded. Dr. John Honsinger, senior veterinary surgeon, was killed some distance away from the ongoing fighting, as was their sutler (who supplied the troops with food), Augustus Baliran, and a Private Ball. General Stanley spoke of this trio being "waylaid and killed"[13] by six Indians. These six Indians were led by Rain-in-the-Face, and it was he who had actually killed Honsinger, later bragging about it and keeping his gold watch. This would come back to haunt him, as he was later arrested by Tom Custer at Standing Rock Reservation for Dr. Honsinger's murder. His escape prevented any retribution for his crime, and he would develop a deep hatred for the Custer brothers, apparently boasting that he would kill Tom Custer and cut out his heart. Rain-in-the-Face and the Custers would meet again along the Little Bighorn River in less than three years.

For the next three days Custer would see glimpses of the Indians, keeping watch of the command as they moved deeper into Indian country. Keeping at a safe distance, the Sioux were in no position to confront the soldiers again—at least, not until it suited them. On August 8, the column was just about opposite the mouth of Rosebud River. General Stanley recalled, "[W]e discovered that a very large Indian village was fleeing before us. Pursuit was resolved upon, and at 9 p.m., Lieut. Col. Custer left with all the cavalry and Indian scouts to try and overtake the village. The troops carried seven days' short rations and 100 rounds of ammunition per man."[14] It is a bit odd that Custer did not request at least a doubling of their ammunition, as they were pursuing a large village, and had almost run out of that most necessary element for survival in their fight of August 4.

In the end, however, it wouldn't matter, for after about a thirty-six-hour chase, they discovered the Indians had "crossed the Yellowstone in skin-boats and rafts three miles below the mouth of the Big Horn River."[15] Despite the valiant efforts of the troops to cross the river, it was impossible due to its depth and the swiftness of its current. The troops' horses, laden down with equipment, were unable to make the crossing. Other measures were tried, such as stringing ropes across, but these failed as well. Understanding and taking advantage of the army's predicament, the Indians attacked them early on the morning of August 11 by directing rifle fire from concealed positions across the river, which was at this point some seven hundred feet wide. Acting more boldly (no doubt enraged that the troopers were following the village), the warriors crossed the river on their ponies both up- and downstream of Custer, planning a full-scale attack from both directions at once. Here again, the situation became precarious, but Custer, a man absolutely born for war, quickly rose to the occasion and dispatched units to meet the threat. As the Sioux had sent hundreds of braves to fight them, it was not simply a tactic to alleviate the pressure, giving the women and children of the village a chance to escape. Rather, the Sioux were intent on destroying the Seventh Cavalry that day along the banks of the Yellowstone River. And while the sight must have been a little disconcerting to the newer recruits, the cavalry quickly gained the upper hand and chased the warriors for as many as ten miles.

General Stanley and the main command reached Custer about 7:00 a.m. that morning, and the view presented to him was one of large groups of Indians gathering on the bluffs across the Yellowstone, out of rifle range. But Stanley had more than rifles with him on the expedition. "I directed Lieutenant Webster, Twenty-Second Infantry, in command of the section of artillery, to shell these groups," Stanley wrote. "[H]e threw several shells, very well aimed, and producing a wonderful scampering out of sight."[16]

So ended what became known as the Battle of the Yellowstone. The remainder of the expedition was rather uneventful, and it would do nothing to subjugate the Sioux. Although more was accomplished than had been with the Hancock Expedition, it had greater and far more lasting negative results. The incursion into Sioux territory was like putting one's hand into a bees' nest. Plenty of swatting had occurred, but most of the bees were left unharmed, and angrier than before. Despite these two battles with the Indians of the Northern Great Plains, Custer, and the military machine in general, did not possess the wisdom to anticipate how difficult the road ahead was going to be. What lay ahead was incomprehensible to most people back east, and the army, whose job it was to enforce what the government (the people) wanted, did not set their sights very far beyond the immediate. The Indians, however, were under no such illusions. They fully understood that whatever time was left for them to conduct their way of life would be granted only through the spilling of blood, and the struggle they now embraced was a fight to the death.

By November, the Custers were at their new home, Fort Abraham Lincoln, just south of present-day Mandan, North Dakota. They had no idea that they were about to enter the last and most significant phase of their lives. Things would seem normal and life would go on, but the course had been set. Destiny was now aligning itself to bring about a climactic end to the life of George Armstrong Custer. That which would transpire during the upcoming summer campaign of 1874—a campaign where Custer was in full command and thus, fully responsible—would be a line of demarcation that, once crossed, would set future events in motion, sealing the fate of the most flamboyant figure to ever wear the military uniform of the United States.

The Black Hills, a relatively small mountain range stretching from western South Dakota into Montana, has been sacred to the Sioux since at least 1776, when they drove the Cheyenne from the region. They would manage to hold on to it for a hundred years. The Black Hills gets its name from the rich collections of trees sprouting from the mountain, giving it a dark, almost black look from afar. Although whites have referred to this area as the Black Hills for years, the Lakota call it *Paha Sapa*, sacred land that was not negotiable. Indeed, the United States government had already given them the right to the land through the Fort Laramie Treaty of 1868. Not only were whites forbidden to settle in this vast and uninhabited region, but they were also forbidden to even travel or pass through it. As far as the Indians were concerned, this was an ironclad agreement. While the US government was about to go back on its word, the validity of the treaty would be upheld one hundred years in the future by the United States Supreme Court.

The expedition that Custer would lead into the Black Hills in 1874 was a turning point for both Indians and whites. Born out of a desire to crush the will of the Sioux, General Philip Sheridan had a plan to damage their enemy. On May 1, 1874, he sent a request to his commander, General William Tecumseh Sherman, stating the need to explore the Black Hills and to establish a fort at an appropriate location. This, of course, was in direct violation of the Fort Laramie Treaty of 1868, which stated that the Black Hills were part of the Great Sioux Reservation,[17] and there's no way Sheridan and Sherman were not aware of it. Sherman quickly agreed to the expedition, and in fact wanted the march to become one giant research project. Sheridan dispatched the following letter to Custer: "It is especially desirable that these Headquarters should have a complete detailed description of the country passed over, so it is desired that you will devote yourself to the collection of such information, and embody it in a daily diary. This should embrace distance travelled, character of the soil, wood, water, and grass, and topography of surface and geological formation. . . ."[18]

It had been rumored for some time that gold was in the Black Hills, and the march being assembled by Sherman and Sheridan, using Custer as the instrument of aggression, would confirm what many had suspected. A stampede of white prospectors—and the merchants and ladies who would cater to them—would forever transform the Black Hills. Indeed, the threat of the Northern Pacific Railroad, and the swarm of people it would bring, paled in comparison to the flood of humanity that was coming to the Black Hills once gold was discovered. There would be no turning back, and while the Sioux would lose control of it, they were not willing to hand it over without exacting a heavy price. The rage Custer would face at the Little Bighorn in late June of 1876 had its real genesis in the Black Hills. He was the one who had come to Paha Sapa, and they would not forget it. The unintended consequences of pushing into the Great Sioux Reservation and the Black Hills was that they were paving the way for the Great Sioux War of 1876–77, in which Custer and his Seventh Cavalry would play a prominent part. But that would not be realized until much later.

During that summer, everything seemed to be going in the right direction for the United States and its interests. The army had not had a disaster in quite some time, and they always enjoyed the summer campaigning. So it was no surprise that Fort Abraham Lincoln began humming with activity that June of 1874, as ten companies of the Seventh Cavalry converged, as did two companies of infantry, as many as seventy-five Indian scouts, as well as a civilian entourage consisting of geologists, two engineers (one civilian, one military), four scientists, three newspaper reporters, three doctors, a photographer, and of course, two mining officials in search of the gold most believed was waiting in the Black Hills, bringing the entire command to nearly one thousand strong. Two names of note going with the command were Lieutenant Frederick D. Grant (son of President Ulysses S. Grant) and Major George A. Forsyth, the commander and hero of Beecher's Island. Custer, understanding the possibilities of a fatal encounter while in Indian country, looked over his life insurance policies, making certain they were still in force so that Libbie would be taken care of if the unexpected became a reality.

Armaments for the campaign consisted of Gatling guns, cannon, and the new Springfield single-shot breech-loading carbine. It was the offspring of the Infantry Springfield rifle, but due to its smaller and lighter construction (just seven pounds), it carried a cartridge sporting a .45 to .55 load rather than the standard .45 to .70 bullet of the rifle. The round packed a great deal of punch, but with one terrible drawback: The copper shell casing would sometimes stick in the breech after the ejector snapped off a piece of the shell's rim, leaving the weapon momentarily inoperable. Although this malfunction could be rather quickly "fixed" by prying the shell casing out with a knife blade, this could be a deadly predicament during battle. This was not a problem with every issued carbine, nor was it a complaint with every trooper, but it did occur in a number of weapons, and it probably cost some terrified troopers their lives.

The command would set off on July 2 with Custer as senior commander of the expedition. How he must have savored that after combating General Stanley during his last foray into the wild. No longer being told what to do, Custer would conduct the expedition as he saw fit. Riding ahead as usual to scout out the land, he nevertheless took great precautions by always having a detachment of at least eighty men and an appropriate number of Indian scouts galloping along with him, as he understood the inherent dangers of being in the middle of Sioux country. There would be no battle with hostile warriors as there had been with the last expedition, where the warriors had shown unusual boldness in trying to kill them. The only battle for the average trooper was in the mind, as the expectation of an Indian attack either day or night was a real possibility. This time, the Indians were completely satisfied with just watching the command. They were apt to pop up at any moment from behind the hills to get a look at the invading column. The sight of the smoke signals being traded by two parties some distance apart turned heads and raised questions with the men as to what they were up to, but an attack would not be forthcoming. This knowledge that the expedition was being "followed" by the Sioux was no doubt a bit nerve-racking as the troopers drifted off to sleep at night, no matter how many pickets Custer placed around the camp.

For Custer, the expedition was an exciting time simply because he was once again in the field, in the uncharted wild, hunting and collecting live specimens of rattlesnakes, foxes, and other creatures of the Northern Great Plains. On July 31, the command reached Harney Peak. With its elevation of 7,244 feet, it was a challenge Custer, the supreme outdoorsman, couldn't resist. Taking several others with him, he began the conquest of the mountain, while the Seventh camped at its base. Throughout the march, traces of gold had been found by the mining team of Horatio Nelson Ross and William McKay. When the first substantial find of gold was discovered on August 1, it would change everything. In a letter dated August 15, 1874, addressed to the Assistant Adjutant General of the Department of the Dakota, Custer wrote: "I referred in a former dispatch to the discovery of gold. Subsequent examinations at numerous points confirm and strengthen the fact of the existence of gold in the Black Hills."[19]

The messenger Custer chose to take this message to the world was none other than his trusted scout, Charley Reynolds. Reynolds, an accomplished scout who understood the ways of the West and the Indians as well as anyone, prepared for his ride by nailing horseshoes on backward in the hope that any Sioux who might be inclined to follow his trail would go in the opposite direction.[20] Galloping through territory teeming with Indians who were willing to kill any white man foolish enough to be caught out there alone, he hid himself during the day in the trees or whatever suitable gully or depression might be available to him. Riding only at night, Reynolds made it to Fort Laramie unscathed, and soon the telegraphed message of gold being found in the Black Hills reached those back east. It was only a matter of time before prospectors from every area would hurry there. Despite even legitimate efforts over the following months by the army to keep out the hordes of prospectors hunting for gold, there just wasn't any way to stop the influx. Even attempts by the government to purchase the land were flatly rejected. It was clear the Indians had no intention of giving up their sacred land, guaranteed them by the Fort Laramie Treaty. Filled with rage, the Sioux took note of all that transpired and would later dub the route Custer took to the Black Hills the "Thieves Road." When the command returned to Fort Abraham Lincoln on August 30, they had covered over eight hundred miles in just sixty days.[21]

With the Black Hills Expedition completed, the Custers would be entering a phase of relative tranquility and peace, where life would be more normal for this famous couple who had now been married ten years. Indeed, it was a time to reflect and enjoy one another, and while it was a period absent of combat for Custer, it was not without its problems. Their two-story home at Fort Abraham Lincoln burned to the ground when a fire erupted in the chimney flue (a better, three-story home was then rapidly built to replace it). Regrettably (in his mind), Custer was prevented from commanding the Black Hills Expedition for the summer of 1875, which meant menial and routine duties at Fort Lincoln—an unpleasant life for a man like Custer. The couple would, however, spend many happy hours at their home with family and friends, and they would visit Monroe.

Custer would also take the time to once again visit New York City, and, like before, he was welcomed and praised by an adoring public. He immediately wrote Libbie to tell her all about it. Again, he toyed with the idea of a life in business, to gain wealth not usually acquired by a career in the army. In his heart, however, he understood his need to be in the saddle, commanding men and following orders in the midst of the military exploits that brought meaning and satisfaction to his life. So, throughout 1874 and 1875, Custer would indulge himself in the social activities of being a husband to Libbie and a friend to those he was comfortable with, and for the last time, he would move about in that familiar world he always retreated to when war was not an option. It was good that he could do so, for at the dawn of 1876, a centennial year for the United States, the vortex of what was coming began to stir, and the unseen forces that would author his demise were already at work. Time was running out for George Armstrong Custer.

⌒⌒

It is of interest to note that the expedition against the Sioux in 1876 nearly occurred without Custer. Custer had been called to testify in Washington, D.C., at the House Committee on Expenditures, concerning the scandals of President Grant's administration—specifically, those concerning Secretary of War William W. Belknap, whose tentacles of deceit and theft stretched in many directions. Custer soon found himself in a bit of trouble. The Grant administration was rife with impropriety from beginning to end and always included friends of the president, and very often, family members as well. Custer's testimony to the committee was without malice, and while he enlightened them as to the areas where he believed abuse existed, he did not expect it to harm his standing with the president. He was wrong. During a recess in the testimony, Custer took the time to write Libbie, referring to the proceedings as being "where the Belknap exposures were brought to light."[22]

Grant did not like anyone tarnishing the reputation of his family and friends, and despite the good feelings Grant obviously had for Custer from his rise as a military icon during the Civil War, he was incensed at Custer's testimony. Of course, even if Custer had not testified concerning these matters, Belknap still would have gone down in flames, so it is a little surprising that Grant would take the step of ordering Custer not to join his beloved Seventh Cavalry for the upcoming campaign with the Sioux. Disregarding good sense, however, this is exactly what he did. When this occurred, even good pal Phil Sheridan said nothing, nor did Sherman, although both desperately wanted Custer in the field, leading his men against the Indians. They believed that if anyone would be able to subjugate them, it would be Custer. If not for the intervention of General Alfred Terry, who was instrumental in changing Grant's mind, Custer would have been left behind.

CHAPTER 9

The Year of Premonitions

The centennial year of 1876 was to be a year of celebration for the United States of America. People across the country were caught up in preparations pertaining to the nation's one hundredth birthday. The deep psychological wounds caused by the Civil War were beginning to heal as leaders from across the country pledged their mutual support. When the mayor of Montgomery, Alabama, M. L. Moses, sent greetings to the centennial commission in Philadelphia, Pennsylvania, he was quick to remind them that while Montgomery was the birthplace of the Confederate government, the city council wanted to extend a "cordial and fraternal greeting to all the people of the United States, with an earnest prayer for the perpetuation of concord and brotherly feeling throughout our land."[1] This language does seem a bit archaic by today's standards, yet when one stops to consider that only eleven years earlier, the sons of Montgomery and the sons of Philadelphia were desperately trying to kill each other, the words take on a special significance.

In the city of Memphis, Tennessee, ex-Confederate and ex-Union artillerymen joined forces for the firing of thirteen cannon, signaling the beginning of festivities for this special July Fourth.[2] This time, however, the booming of the big guns would not be followed by the screams of the wounded and the destruction of property, something the South had had quite enough of. Even so, the sounds of the guns cascading across the city must have caused some of the residents to shudder and recall the horrors once again.

From New York to San Francisco, America had been gearing up for the lavish affair. Philadelphia was the actual hub of activity, as dignitaries from around the world gathered for the huge party, which included an exposition filled with hundreds of exhibits featuring the latest technological wonders of Western man. Even Custer took the time to stop by on his way to New York on April 20. This was going to be a special summer, and every white person old enough to understand knew it.

Not all Americans were sharing in the revelry, for the Native Americans had little to celebrate as they confronted the ever-growing power of the white world. The Sioux, already enraged by the incursion into the Black Hills, were enjoying their freedom and were determined to hang on to it. Indeed, they would have their own time of celebration—not in cities and towns like their enemy, but out on the Great Plains. It would be here, on a barren Montana field, that a series of events would culminate, and the summer of joy would quickly dissolve into the summer of violence. The year 1876 would prove to be a drastic time of change for both cultures.

The turning point was a meeting that occurred at the White House on September 3, 1875. By this time over fifteen thousand prospectors had invaded the Black Hills, not to mention the throngs of people who had followed them. The meeting, presided over by President Grant himself, and including generals Philip Sheridan and George Crook, was nothing more than the formulation of a strategy to overwhelm and conquer the Sioux, the Northern Cheyenne, and any other Indians who refused to leave the Great Plains behind and enter a reservation. There could be no more roving bands of Indians, regardless of tribe, and the life they had once known was now over. The matter was turned over to the War Department for what the Grant administration believed was the final solution to the Indian problem. The hopes and dreams of Sheridan, Sherman, and even Grant rested on George Armstrong Custer, and there was little doubt in their minds he would conquer the Sioux just as he had the Cheyenne along the Washita. There could be no other outcome.

The government had decreed that all non-treaty Indians were to come onto the reservation by January 31, 1876. All Indian agents were informed and were to pass the word along to the Indians so they could get the word out to those on the Plains. Of course, it was absurd of the government to expect the Indians to respond in such a short time. Not only was it wintertime, but the lack of communication between those on the reservation and the bands of Indians scattered out in the wild meant that it was virtually impossible for all of the non-treaty Indians to even hear of the demand. That was the point: Neither the Grant administration nor the top brass of the army were interested any longer in placating Indian demands. They couldn't come right out and say it, but it was clear that they now preferred a war in which the Sioux, Cheyenne, and all Indians they considered hostile would be soundly defeated in battle, so that complete subjugation could occur. The Indians had become an annoyance, and these former Civil War veterans, hardened by the life they had led, would do to the Indians what they never would have done to the Confederates. It was a war of race and culture, and because the momentum was clearly with them, they would take advantage of it. Custer, who had far more respect for Indians than did Sheridan or Sherman, was chosen to do their bidding.

The actual campaign against Sitting Bull's Sioux and the Northern Cheyenne would involve several columns of troops in what was to be, more or less, a search-and-destroy mission. It would be what military tacticians call a pincer movement, or, in perhaps even more physical terms, hammer and anvil. Sheridan wanted this grand battle with the Indians to occur during the winter months, when the warriors were not at their best. Custer, having already proven how adept he was at winter warfare, would have good success, Sheridan believed. However, bringing together such a large contingent of troops (cavalry, infantry, and artillery) would be no easy task, and would take time. Sheridan's desire to engage in a winter war would not come off as expected. Indeed, the entire campaign would encounter trouble from the very start.

This three-pronged attack would involve the combined efforts of General George Crook's (Department of the Platte) detachment, departing Fort Fetterman in southeast Wyoming and heading north in their hunt for the Sioux, while Colonel John Gibbon (District of Montana) would march east with his troops from Fort Ellis. Brigadier General Alfred H. Terry (Department of Dakota), with Custer and the Seventh Cavalry in tow, would launch from Fort Abraham Lincoln in North Dakota. Not everyone would be heading out into the wilds at the same time, of course.

The first steps of this punitive campaign were hampered from the beginning. Indeed, what would take place was but a foreshadowing of things to come. Here you had a combined army, made up almost exclusively of officers who'd honed their combat skills during the Civil War and who were in 1876 using the best and most technological weapons available at that time, and yet they were still at a disadvantage in their war with the Sioux.

During the months of April and May, Colonel John Gibbon combed the wilds north of the Yellowstone River and made initial contact with the Sioux. In fact, Gibbon's chief of scouts, Lieutenant James H. Bradley, during a reconnaissance, located a large Indian village on the Tongue River and reported back to Gibbon, who immediately made plans to attack. However, the Yellowstone proved to be far more daunting than the Indians, and after several unsuccessful attempts to cross the river, the plans were scrubbed. The Indian camp, knowing of the soldiers' presence, moved to another location. Not only was Gibbon prevented from launching a full-fledged attack on the Sioux camp, but warriors (who had no difficulty crossing the river on their ponies) had been dispatched from the village to harass Gibbon. These assaults on Gibbon's forces, which in reality were little more than annoyances, stopped entirely after May 23. Oddly, Gibbon never dispatched a courier to his superior, Brigadier General Alfred Terry, to keep him abreast of any hostile activity he'd encountered.[3] This failure, as well as other failures in communication, would play a large role in the final events at Little Bighorn.

General Crook was actually the first to move out of Fort Fetterman against the Sioux. Leaving the warm confines of the fort behind, Crook and his almost nine hundred men marched out to meet their enemy on March 1, although it would not be much of a contest at the start. The

Indians were adept at communicating with each other by way of smoke signals, which meant that the ever-watchful warriors were aware of the army's intentions and were spreading the word to others. Because of this, along with a successful night raid by a war party to stampede the live-stock, Crook determined that he would have to cut the ten companies of cavalry loose if he had any chance of finding the Indians. He did this by way of a ruse: Making a show of marching to Fort Reno, now abandoned, he waited until the next day and ordered Colonel Joseph J. Reynolds to race ahead with the cavalry to locate the hostiles.[4] Utilizing the well-developed skills of Reynolds's scout, Frank Grouard, they gave chase to a village they knew was out there.

Although it was inching toward springtime, the command was met with a terrible snowstorm and bitterly cold temperatures, which made it rough going for both man and beast. Even so, Grouard's value as a scout was once again confirmed with the discovery of the much-sought-after Cheyenne camp, situated along the Powder River. The village was subse-quently struck, but unlike Custer's attack along the Washita, Reynolds failed to completely surround the village, and while he put the Indians to flight, he did not fully destroy the encampment once it was captured. The Indians were able to recover many of their personal items, including most of their ponies. Like Custer's abandonment of Major Elliott along the Washita, Reynolds's fear of the unknown caused him to abandon the camp without adequately destroying it. Unlike Custer, however, his failure to actually destroy what he'd captured translated into an abject failure. General Crook and company returned to Fort Fetterman without damag-ing the Sioux and Cheyenne. Crook would soon try again, but his second attempt to launch a campaign to subdue the hostiles would be no more successful than the first.

An able soldier, Crook was being buffeted by the winds of war, and no effort on his part—including a change of tactics—was going to alter his course. Defeat lay in his future, but he didn't understand that as his com-mand marched out of Fort Fetterman on May 29. With his unit of just over a thousand men (both cavalry and infantry), Crook was determined to strike a blow at the enemy and complete the task. He was feeling somewhat responsible for Reynolds's poor showing (Reynolds would be court-martialed for his aborted attack on the village). Crook's top scout, Grouard, and the Crow scouts were not a part of the expedition as they marched north toward the ruins of Fort Reno, one of the forts along the Bozeman Trail the government had relinquished per a treaty agreement with the Indians.[5] Not having anyone who could adequately lead them through the wilderness, Crook's column became lost in the days ahead, and it wasn't until June 9, while they were encamped along the Tongue River, that Sioux and Cheyenne warriors attacked them. As one author has written, "Although Crook's casualties were insignificant, the attack was clear evidence that the Indians were in the area and prepared to fight."[6] On June 11, Crook made a permanent encampment near present-day Sheridan, Wyoming. On June 14, Grouard made an appearance with 261 Indian guides (Crow and Shoshone), which was of the utmost importance to the command.

Wanting to strike quickly, Crook ordered the infantry to mount up on mules and join the cavalry. Traveling as light as possible, they left camp around 6:00 a.m. on June 16, each man carrying only one hundred rounds of ammunition (one would think they would have learned by now). Reaching a swampy area around 7:00 p.m. that night, his command of some 1,300 troops, Indian scouts, and civilians made camp not far from Rosebud Creek. As he had done the previous day, Crook had his men up and moving by 3:00 a.m., and by 6:00 a.m. they were marching northward, following the Rosebud. Allowing the men to rest two hours later, the command had little concern that the Sioux and Cheyenne were anywhere nearby, and apparently, little thought was given to the setting out of pickets, as the Shoshone and Crow had gone ahead to the high ground in front of the column. Not even the sound of sporadic firing from the direction of the scouts disturbed anyone. It was merely believed that the guides were shooting at buffalo or other game. It was only when the gunfire grew heavier and one of the scouts was seen running back toward the soldiers, screaming at the top of his lungs, "Lakota, Lakota!"

that everyone understood the battle was now on. Crook's 250-plus Indian scouts fought as they retreated back to the main command, thereby giving the troops a little time to prepare for the assault.

Sending detachments to seize the high ground on both sides, giving them a more-horizontal angle of fire at the Sioux, the command set the soldiers up to begin the first counterattack of the day. The battle would rage for the next six hours as the Indians gave ground and then shifted a portion of their attack to an isolated group on one of the ridges. It was soon clear to Crook that this assault was no ordinary Indian tactic of hit and run, but a sustained assault that would have devastating consequences should his men run out of ammunition—a very real possibility given the long duration of the battle. While the army was successful in repulsing the Indians with each assault, they failed to conquer them or wear them out. Even as the battle was in its final moments, the men had to endure sniping from the ridges from various sun-baked warriors who hadn't grown weary of killing these blue-coats. As Crook's men left the field, they were low on ammunition and glad to be retreating. The cost of the battle to them was thirty-two dead and thirty-one wounded. Reported estimates of Indian casualties that day are anywhere from under twenty to well over one hundred.

Although from a tactical perspective there appeared little advantage to either side after the last shot was fired, it was a clear victory for the Sioux and Cheyenne once George Crook left the field and returned to his base camp along Big Goose Creek. Indeed, it energized the warriors, for they had defeated a large contingent of troops. This victory would fuel their confidence when they met Custer along the Little Bighorn eight days later.

Meanwhile, in mid-June, Chief Sitting Bull held a sun dance, a ritual considered to be one of the most sacred of the Sioux. For several days the famous medicine man, now middle-aged, subjected himself to the rigors and strains of the dance, and on the third day he received what he would later describe as a vision of soldiers falling headlong into camp. For Sitting Bull this could only mean one thing: Any soldiers foolish enough to attack his village would be utterly destroyed. Had Custer heard about

Sitting Bull's vision before he reached the Little Bighorn, he no doubt would have scoffed at it. He had always believed in the invincibility of his regiment, regardless of the size of the opposing force. This was a line of thinking deeply engrained within him based on his miraculous survival during the Civil War and his ability (in his mind) to always make the right choice tactically during the ever-shifting tide of battle.

Even so, during this campaign, Custer would have his own moments of doubt, albeit unspoken ones. Indeed, many who followed him into the valley of the Little Bighorn on that hot Sunday of June 25, 1876, would also have doubts and deep reservations as to what the outcome of the campaign might be. But like automatons, they could only follow their leader, and very little would be said among them. It is a strange dichotomy, but while the Sioux rejoiced in their freedom on the Great Plains, thrilled at the defeat of Crook and confident in their ability to do it again if the need arose, the soldiers attached to Custer entered into a period of doom and dreadful anticipation. This feeling that something terrible was going to happen—a sentiment shared by soldiers and their family members alike—would prove to be all too prophetic, as if a warning was being offered to turn back while it was still possible.

When the Seventh Cavalry marched out of Fort Abraham Lincoln on the morning of May 17, it did so enveloped in this aforementioned sense of doom. General Terry even used the occasion to bolster the spirits of the families by assembling the troops in parade formation, accompanied, of course, by the ever-present band delivering its grand send-off. Just as Sitting Bull felt certain that his prediction of disaster for the US Army would come true, many who witnessed this particular send-off also believed that disaster was on the horizon for Custer and his beloved Seventh Cavalry. Recalling the scene years later, Libbie wrote: "Mothers, with strange eyes, held out their young ones . . . for one last look at their departing fathers . . . the grief of these women was audible and was accompanied by desponding gestures."[7]

Despite the disconcerting alarm among the women, 925 troops trotted out in a formal, two-abreast column, followed by supporting supply wagons and mule trains loaded with ammunition. Also traveling with the command were forty Indian scouts and several white scouts and interpreters, as well as a number of civilians, among them Custer's brother, Boston, and his nephew, Arthur Reed.

Libbie, along with Custer's sister, Mrs. James Calhoun, was allowed to accompany the regiment on its first day's march. Early in the afternoon, camp was made on the Heart River. When the command saddled up and marched out the following morning, Libbie recounts how a certain event intensified her fears. After breaking camp, while the sunlight was still penetrating the morning mist, an odd sight appeared that would again prove prophetic for the Seventh Cavalry. "Soon the bright sun began to penetrate this veil and dispel the haze," Libbie wrote, ". . . and a scene of wonder and beauty appeared." This thing of beauty turned out to be a mirage in which the column appeared to rise from the earth and "thenceforth for a little distance it marched equally plain to the sight on the earth and in the sky."[8]

From this moment onward, Libbie's apprehension became more acute and would continue to grow without letup. Even her usual activities provided no relief, and she, along with many others, would remain within this cloud of despair until the news of the disaster finally reached them. The emotional state of the women was particularly fragile on June 25, the day of the battle. While their husbands were fighting for their lives, a number of women gathered in the Custer home to sing hymns, but this also failed to drive away their inner fears. One woman became so overwhelmed that she collapsed onto the floor, and when someone came to her aid, she buried her head in the woman's lap. Libbie recalled, "All were absorbed in the same thoughts, and their eyes were filled with far-away visions." Only later would she learn that their fears were justified, for at that very hour, "the souls of those we thought upon were ascending to their maker."[9]

Charley Reynolds, known to be a fearless and accomplished scout, was having his own reservations about the upcoming campaign. Having been employed with the Seventh for a number of years, Reynolds was chosen to accompany the regiment on the Little Bighorn Expedition. Having been on many forays into the wilds, this should have been seen by "Lonesome Charley" as just one more adventure. Instead, he was having some very bad feelings about the upcoming campaign. According to Fred Girard, an interpreter with the Seventh, Reynolds twice confided in him that he expected to die during the expedition. Girard advised him to go and see General Terry, knowing that as a civilian, Reynolds might be excused. But Girard said Terry "shamed him out of it."[10] Reynolds would die shortly after the first shots of this battle were fired. Had he been a little more forceful with Terry, he would have been spared this untimely death.

As for Custer, there was no observable anxiety on his part as he said good-bye to his precious Libbie at the Heart River camp a day earlier. Yet the grief being expressed by the families at Fort Abraham Lincoln must have had an effect on him, and his men as well. It would be just four days before his death that Custer would experience the same type of trepidation that had engulfed those he bid farewell to at the start of this campaign.

On June 21 the Seventh was camped along the mouth of the Rosebud. Here, Custer, along with General Terry and Colonel Gibbon, engaged in a conference aboard the steamer *Far West*—the same steamer which would, in just a very few days, carry the wounded and the survivors away from the slaughter. Major Marcus Reno, at General Terry's orders, had conducted a reconnaissance with six cavalry companies, to search for signs of the Indians and where they might be heading. The results of his scouting had revealed that the most likely location to catch them would be along the Little Bighorn River. (Custer, who always wanted to be out front, was irritated that Terry had chosen Reno for the mission, as he felt himself far more qualified.)

It was during this time, after the final plans had been formulated, that Custer would emerge a changed man. His former confidence in his invincibility pertaining to matters of war was abruptly replaced with an unspoken sense of doom. Indeed, this mysterious bleak cloud seems to have floated over the entire command. Letters were written and wills were made, remembers Lieutenant Godfrey, who felt that his fellow officers must have had a "presentiment of their fate."[11] No such feelings engulfed

General Terry, however, as he believed Custer could handle himself in battle.

At noon on June 22, the Seventh broke camp and continued their march up the Rosebud and toward their destiny. Before their departure, Custer was offered the Second Cavalry to accompany the expedition but unwisely rejected them. His reason for passing on this additional fire-power, he said, was that the Seventh could handle anything it came up against. In Custer's mind, the regiment was both omnipotent and immortal. When he was offered the use of at least two Gatling guns (the fore-runner of the machine gun, the most devastating weapon ever produced for use against ground troops), his response was the same. The refusal of the wheeled Gatling guns may have been purely logistical, as transport-ing them may have been too difficult and certainly would have slowed him down. But saying no to the extra cavalry was no doubt born out of his pride that the regiment, under his direct leadership, was sufficient for anything the Sioux had to offer. Frederick Benteen, never a fan of Custer's, wrote to his wife, saying: "Had Custer carried out the orders he got from Genl. Terry, the command would have formed a junction exactly at the village, and have captured the whole of tepees, etc., and probably any quantity of squaws, papooses, etc. but Custer disobeyed orders from the fact of not wanting any other command—or body to have a finger in the pie—and thereby lost his life."[12]

At 4:00 p.m. on June 22, the regiment halted the column and made camp. Custer was now twelve miles closer to battle. At dusk, the offi-cers' call was sounded, and Custer, still immersed in his invisible cloud of dread, began relating to his officers in a most unusual way. "This 'talk' of his," remembered Lieutenant Godfrey, "was considered at the time something extraordinary for General Custer, for it was not his habit to unbosom himself to his officers. In it he showed a lack of confidence, a reliance on somebody else; there was an indefinable something that was not Custer."[13] This, of course, had a profound effect on those gath-ered around their leader, and such an odd expression of his personality no doubt heightened their own fears as well. As Godfrey and Lieutenant

Wallace turned away from Custer and began walking back to their respective areas, Wallace blurted out: "Godfrey, I believe General Custer is going to be killed." When Godfrey asked him why he felt this way, Wallace responded, "Because I have never heard Custer talk in that way before."[14] The caution lights were now flashing in every direction for the Seventh Cavalry, but to no effect.

Even as Custer inwardly brooded about the way he felt and what it may have meant, the knowledge of what had happened to the Crook expedition was unknown to him. He was also unaware of the Sioux warrior who went by the name of Crazy Horse, the part he had played in the battle along the Rosebud, and the fact that the two were due to meet in just a matter of days. While Custer was going to die without this knowledge of Crook's defeat, he would have plenty of voices around him that were quite knowledgeable of the enemy's strength and were constantly warning him of the dangers that lay ahead.

Mitch Boyer, the famous half-breed scout (his father was French, his mother a full-blooded Sioux), had been loaned to Custer by Colonel Gibbon and would ultimately perish with the doomed command. With some thirty years' experience on the Great Plains, Custer should have weighed carefully Boyer's advice concerning the number of Sioux they were likely to face, for Boyer's assessment was exactly the same as that of Custer's trusted scout, Bloody Knife. Indeed, on the last morning of their lives, Bloody Knife told Custer that there were more Sioux awaiting them than they had bullets. This matter-of-fact statement would not deter Custer from his imagined triumph over the Indians; in fact, Bloody Knife's warning bounced off Custer like bullets ricocheting off a stone wall. How tragic it must have been for those offering the warnings to have Custer respond in such a manner, yet there was nothing they could do about it.

Custer's failure to heed the advice of his Indian scouts at this critical moment may be due in part to his strong belief that the white person's interpretation of the facts, militarily speaking, was always superior to that of the Indians'. A case in point would be Custer's failure to believe his Osage scouts who detected the odor of fire just before the attack on Black

Kettle's camp. Only when the remains of the fire were discovered did Custer and the white officers believe them. Custer would learn that his scouts were accurate in this case, as well, but by the time this was discovered, it would be too late. To his detriment, Custer believed all Indians, friendly or hostile, were unable to grasp the kind of concepts about tactics and war that he had learned at West Point, and as such, felt that white soldiers were under no real threat when in sufficient numbers, no matter how many enraged warriors they might be facing. One can easily assume (and correctly so) that this was a form of racism, if unintentional—a part of the culture of the times. Custer's refusal to listen to those who knew better turned out to be both a costly and fatal mistake.

When Custer asked Fred Girard his opinion concerning the number of hostiles they were likely to encounter, Girard responded "Not less than twenty-five hundred,"[15] an estimate fully one thousand higher than Custer may have expected to meet. Custer having sought out Girard's advice, one might be inclined to think that Girard's higher figure would have sparked the necessary caution within Custer, slowing him down somewhat, giving him time to take a second look at the situation. Yet none of this would occur.

At 5:00 a.m. on the morning of June 23, the command was on the move, marching up the Rosebud. Because of the slow-moving pack train, the regiment was obliged to halt after a trek of only fifteen miles. Signs of large Indian movements were everywhere, and before the day's march was completed they would pass the remains of three different hostile camps, each ranging in diameter from a third- to a half-mile wide. Still, Custer could not perceive the dangers that lay like coiled snakes just ahead, and it must have appeared to the Indians, who were aware of their presence, that Sitting Bull's vision of the US Army's destruction would indeed come to pass.

The several-hundred-yard-wide trail that the troops followed on June 23 was enlarged by the next day to a half-mile, and was very fresh.[16] The ground the Seventh was crossing was quite rough in spots, the bluffs being broken, which caused the regiment to follow a meandering course in their trek into the valley.[17] By the end of the day the command had covered approximately thirty-three miles. The march of June 24 brought Custer to an abandoned camp much larger than the ones previously encountered. At this camp, however, there stood a "sun dance" lodge that contained the scalp of a white man, no doubt from one of Colonel Gibbon's men, killed several weeks earlier. Here Custer gathered together his officers to discuss the situation. It was during this gathering that a strange, and to some, disturbing, incident occurred, viewed as a bad omen for the Seventh Cavalry. "At this time a stiff southerly breeze was blowing," recalled Lieutenant Godfrey. "As we were about to separate, the General's headquarters flag was blown down, falling to our rear. Being near the flag I picked it up and stuck the staff in the ground, but it fell again to the rear."[18]

The falling of the flag was yet another sign, or one more fearful omen, for those already troubled about what was waiting for them as the Seventh Cavalry neared its destination. It was a road into uncharted territory, and it was starting to feel like a road of no return.

The scouts, who were being quite thorough in their search, were paying special attention to the area around Tulloch's Creek. By day's end the command had marched some twenty-eight miles, finally making camp around sundown, behind the cover of a bluff. The troops, both tired and saddle-weary, would not be permitted to rest long. By 11:30 p.m. the command was once again on the move in pursuit of the Sioux and would not rest again until 2:30 a.m. The degree of exhaustion for the average solder at this time cannot be overstated. Besides the knowledge that an upcoming battle was a certainty (and a surprise attack on them could occur anytime), the endless marching, the heat, and the overall depravation of even the most basic comforts of life at the average fort in the West were hard to endure for all the troops, but especially for those raw recruits experiencing their first expedition. By 3:00 a.m. the sleepy men were allowed to make coffee, but even this simple pleasure was spoiled, as the water was quite alkaline. "We almost gagged on it," remembered Private Charles Windolph of Company H.[19]

Instead of dismounting with the others at 2:30 a.m., Lieutenant Charles Varnum and his scouts were arriving at the spot known as the

Crow's Nest. This is where the command would catch their first glimpse of the great Sioux encampment they would soon attack. The Indians were camping in the valley of the Little Bighorn, merely conducting their daily routine. Any disturbance of their lives would guarantee trouble, and then the battle would begin. Within hours, George Armstrong Custer and his men of the Seventh Cavalry would rise to the sound of "Boots and Saddles." For many, it was the last time they would answer that call.

Even though it was Custer's intention to draw as close as possible to the large Indian village, while remaining undetected, and attack on June 26 as planned, circumstances would dictate otherwise. The time for premonitions was almost over. The stark reality of the situation, like a brilliant flash, was about to engulf all the players in this strange morality play. The mighty Seventh Cavalry, with Custer at its head, was experiencing its last moment of pride as the most revered cavalry regiment of the army. They were transitioning to another type of glory, where they would forever be enshrined in a battle destined to be remembered. They were making history, but not in the ways they had imagined.

Major General George Armstrong Custer, April 1865
COURTESY OF THE LIBRARY OF CONGRESS, LC-DIG-CWPB-05341

Custer, sitting with pistol on lap during the Peninsula Campaign, May 1862
COURTESY OF THE LIBRARY OF CONGRESS, LC-DIG-CWPB-01007

Custer, reclining for the camera during the Peninsula Campaign of 1862

President Lincoln visiting his officers soon after the battle of Antietam, Maryland, fought in September 1862; Captain Custer stands at far right.

Taking a break from war, an uncharacteristically weary-looking Custer poses hatless for the camera. COURTESY OF THE LIBRARY OF CONGRESS, LC-DIG-CWPBH-03122

George and Libbie Custer, circa 1864
COURTESY OF THE LIBRARY OF CONGRESS, LC-BH831-702B

Sheridan and his generals

George, Libbie, and
Tom Custer, 1864

Custer, sitting for the camera
in New York

Custer triumphant, 1865

General Custer, sporting
an expression forged in
war, 1865

Adventure on the
Great Plains, 1868
COURTESY OF LITTLE
BIGHORN BATTLEFIELD
NATIONAL MONUMENT

Custer and Libbie dining in the field
COURTESY OF LITTLE BIGHORN BATTLEFIELD NATIONAL MONUMENT

Chief Red Cloud, who "won" the war along the Bozeman Trail

Wielding the pen under the watchful eyes of wife Libbie at Fort Abraham Lincoln
COURTESY OF LITTLE BIGHORN BATTLEFIELD NATIONAL MONUMENT

Major Marcus A. Reno
COURTESY OF LITTLE
BIGHORN BATTLEFIELD
NATIONAL MONUMENT

Albert and Jennie Barnitz
COURTESY OF LITTLE BIGHORN BATTLEFIELD NATIONAL
MONUMENT

Captain Frederick Benteen

Custer (reclining on ground) with his Seventh Cavalry officers in the Black Hills, 1874. His trusted scout, Bloody Knife, stands behind him; brother Tom is third man from the left, and Captain Frederick Benteen is third man from the right.

Custer kills a grizzly outside of camp, the Black Hills, 1874; Bloody Knife is to his right, Tom Custer kneels beside him.

Sitting Bull, the great Sioux chief whose vision of soldiers falling headlong into camp came to pass

Chief Gall, who later admitted his heart became "bad" during the Custer fight

General George Crook

Custer Hill as it appeared in 1894

CHAPTER 10

Valley of Fear

A little before 8:00 a.m. on the last morning of his life, George Armstrong Custer was summoned to the Crow's Nest to see for himself the hostile camp that awaited them. Not even waiting to saddle up his horse, he rode Vic bareback throughout the camp, spouting orders to the various officers in charge. Custer was dressed in a blue-gray flannel shirt, buckskin trousers, and long cavalry boots. Although his hair was already short, he trimmed it even further for this campaign. Gone were the long locks he had worn during the Civil War. On this particular morning he was seen wearing a regular company hat.[1] By 8:30 the Seventh was up and moving, and the gloom which had been so prevalent with the troops was finally fading away. In fact, despite being tired and saddle-sore, many of the men were now joking with one another and feeling more confident than they had in days.[2]

After a very short march lasting little more than an hour, the regiment halted, and the troops concealed themselves in a ravine. It was Custer's intention to keep the regiment out of sight and attack the village in the early morning hours of June 26, repeating the spectacular surprise he'd visited upon Black Kettle's camp along the Washita. Custer, not wanting to waste any time, galloped off to the Crow's Nest where he could personally view his prize. Ascending to the location where he could obtain the best view, Custer raised the field glasses to his eyes but could not detect the village. No matter how carefully he steadied himself, he just couldn't see it. Here again, Custer was warned by the scouts just how large a village they were about to do battle with, but because he didn't see it himself, he doubted it was there. Perhaps this dilemma was due to the fact that Custer viewed the camp later in the morning when the sun was rising in the sky, and the advancing heat of the day had begun to produce a haze, thereby distorting the images before him.[3] Whatever it was, Custer refused to believe the Indians were there, and the Sioux and Cheyenne would benefit from his "blindness." Captain Frederick Benteen, however, did believe it, saying "I'd sooner trust the sharp eye of an Indian than to trust a pretty good binocular."[4]

Bloody Knife, destined to die along with his leader, gave Custer one final warning, begging him to use extreme caution, but this too was ignored, as Custer had now become little more than a pied piper, leading his troops to an early grave. After additional information was brought to him that some Indians had recovered a hardtack box which had fallen off a pack mule, he believed the element of surprise had now been lost. This assumption may have been incorrect, as later reports indicate that the two or three Indians who were seen trying to open the box did not return to the village. In any event, believing his prize might soon slip away, Custer ordered his bugler to sound out the "officers' call." When the shrill sound of the bugle pierced the air, the entire command realized something was afoot, as no bugle calls had been allowed during the past two days' march. The bugler, an Italian immigrant-turned-soldier by the name of Giovanni Martini, stated that the officers came to Custer in a hurry and that the enlisted men were kept away.[5]

Believing now that every Sioux and Cheyenne in the valley of the Little Bighorn was now learning of their presence, Custer decided to attack immediately. This decision would not necessarily have proven fatal, but it would mean that the Seventh Cavalry, greatly outnumbered, would be forced to fight without the assistance of the Gibbon and Terry columns. Unbeknownst to Custer, but soon to be realized, was the actual size of the encampment that lay sprawled in the valley of the Little Bighorn. Even so, it would be the accumulation of bad decisions which would dig the grave for the Seventh Cavalry.

As the regiment proceeded into the valley of the Little Bighorn, they were passing the point of no return. History was being made, but at a very high cost. It is an absolute certainty that many following Custer that hot day, especially the newer recruits, were convinced that the boy general, who had led them into the wilderness, would also lead them out again. After all, this had always been the result of every battle Custer participated in. Everyone serving under him clearly understood that while any one of them might die in battle, Custer would survive the encounter, for this is how it had always been. For many, Custer and victory were one and the same. But the Indians, in far greater strength than Custer believed, and in no mood to be bullied into submission, would today gain a victory over the whites that no one thought possible. Wanting only to be left alone, the Sioux would not be so forgiving of those who had brought fire and lead to their doorsteps. As Benteen would later say, "We were at their hearths and homes, their medicine was working well, and they were fighting for all the good God gives anyone to fight for."[6]

The camp that Custer thought would flee at the first sign of trouble was, by some estimates, the largest Indian gathering to ever occur on the North American Plains, and was perhaps as much as one to one and a half miles in length. Highly organized, the various tribes camped in order, always retaining the same position relative to one another after every move. It was, so to speak, the Indian version of a city on wheels. Occupying the lower end of the village were the Hunkpapa Sioux. Next were the Sans Arc, followed by the Miniconjou, Blackfoot Sioux, Santee Sioux, Yankton, Oglala (from which Crazy Horse would spring), and the Brule. Comprising the northern end of the camp were the famous fighters, the Cheyenne. It would be here at the Cheyenne camp that Custer would present himself like a lamb to the slaughter. Did he remember the 1869 promise from the medicine man that death would take him should he ever again attack the Cheyenne? Of this we can only speculate, for any white man unfortunate enough to survey the scene did not live to tell about it. The Cheyenne, of course, were delighted to have the opportunity to keep their promise, and the Sioux were very eager to help them.

At approximately 12:20 p.m., Custer made the fatal decision to split the command. By doing so, he ensured his own defeat. As he was under the impression that his presence had been discovered, he fully expected the Indians to flee. This was his worst fear, for he knew just how adept the Indians were in their ability to quickly break camp and disappear over the horizon. This is why the army constantly had to employ Indians in the pursuit of other Indians. The first to be dispatched was Captain Benteen. Earlier in the day, when Custer, Benteen, the scout Charley Reynolds, and several other officers were gathered together, Private Charles Windolph overheard Reynolds warning them concerning the size of the camp they were about to attack. During the conversation, Windolph heard Benteen say to Custer, "Hadn't we [better] keep the regiment together, General? If this is as big a camp as they say, we'll need every man we have."[7] But Custer, whose mind was now closed like a steel trap, and whose destruction was completely assured, could only utter, "You have your orders."[8]

Benteen understood the order was foolish before the general had uttered the last word, but orders were orders. As he would later testify, he was told "to proceed out into a line of bluffs about four or five miles away, to pitch into anything I came across and to send back word."[9] After Benteen and his three companies had traveled about one mile, a rider brought word that if he had discovered nothing thus far, he was to continue his march to the second line of bluffs. After another mile, a second rider caught up with him, informing him of Custer's wish that if he still had seen no sign of the enemy after the second line of bluffs, he was to continue into the valley, and if still nothing had been found, he was to proceed into the next valley.[10]

In Benteen's mind, his trek to the left would take his command away from the main body at a forty-five-degree angle to only God knew where. Under Benteen's immediate command were companies H, D, and K. He would later describe the ground over which they marched as "very rugged."[11] Private Windolph said the hills they were forced to cross were "pitching and bucking as far as you could see."[12] Soon after this, Custer ordered Major Marcus Reno to take companies A, G, and M. This left Custer with companies C, E, F, I, and L under his direct command. Captain McDougall, in charge of the slow-moving but vital pack train, would meander into the chaos later that afternoon.

Although separated, the Reno-Custer columns would travel together for some distance, and would not split up until Reno attacked the village. At that time, Custer and his five companies would ascend the high bluffs (where Reno would soon retreat), so as to flank the village in some capacity known only to himself. When they arrived at the spot known as the Lone Tepee, which contained the remains of a warrior who had been killed in the fight with Crook, events began to quicken. From this point, the two commands would separate forever. Fred Girard, who had advanced to a hill some forty or fifty yards from the dead Indian's lodge, was able to see a part of the village, as well as a pony herd. "Then I hollered to General Custer," Girard said, "here are your Indians, running like devils."[13] As a number of Indians were seen fleeing toward the Little Bighorn, and because scouts from the Rees tribe would not pursue them, Custer ordered Reno to give chase. Several miles in the distance lay Custer's prize, and already dust could be seen rising above the village as Sitting Bull's people made preparations for their safety.

Reno's orders, which were sent to him through Custer's adjutant, William W. Cooke, were quite clear: He was to cross the river and attack the hostile camp, and Custer would support him with the entire command. This promise of direct support was obviously taken literally by Reno, and by the other officers as well. English was English, and this is what Custer said. Once the first shots were fired, Reno fully and correctly expected Custer and his five companies to come sweeping down into the valley, and through this *combined* effort, they would destroy the Sioux and Cheyenne encampment. When this didn't happen, another sequence of events—a mini debacle, if you will—began to unfold, unraveling the Seventh Cavalry in a most humiliating way. Meanwhile, Benteen kept moving in a "left oblique" over ground no sane Indian would travel, and McDougall, carrying the most important item for any battle—the ammunition—would soon be so far in the rear that his ability to supply the command once the shooting began would come to a screeching halt.

Soon the galloping command would reach the banks of the Little Bighorn River, where it would then cross into the valley and into the jaws of the Sioux. Before crossing the river, however, the column all but halted so as to allow the extremely thirsty horses to drink from the cool stream. Wisely, a number of troops bent down and submerged their canteens in the cool water, filling them to the top. Others were not so concerned, but would come to understand the wisdom of it the next day.

Before Reno had completed his task of getting his troops across the river, which at that point did not exceed twenty-five feet in width, the scouts shouted an excited warning that the Sioux were coming to meet them. When Reno heard this, he dispatched a messenger to Custer, informing him of the situation. By doing so, Reno sealed the poor sergeant's fate, as he was never heard from again. The interpreter, Fred Girard, sent a warning as well, telling Lieutenant William Cooke and Captain Myles Keogh, both of whom had been riding with Reno's troops toward the battle. By the time Keogh and Cooke reached Custer, he had stopped to water the horses at the stream known today as Reno Creek. And while we know this word of warning reached Custer, the promise of direct support would not be forthcoming. Disintegration would now tear at Reno's three companies, and total annihilation awaited those racing ahead with Custer.

After crossing the river, Reno led his troops down the valley. Custer, having turned in a northerly direction, rode along the bluffs, and would have been able to see Reno as he quickly approached his moment of battle. Here, too, Custer would gain his first real view—albeit a partial one—of the hostile village. Of course, had it been his intention to support Reno as he engaged the Indians, now would have been the time to do so. Yet given his mode of thinking, and how he desired to alter battle plans according to what he saw going on around him, it is not at all surprising that he did not return. Not only was this decision to prove disastrous, but his failure to include his staff in any evolving tactical developments, birthing additional battle plans, would be nothing short of suicidal. Benteen, ever critical of Custer, later testified that he believed Custer had no plan, and that if he did, he kept it to himself.

It was just shy of 3:00 p.m. when Reno's three companies charged down the valley of the Little Bighorn. Sergeant Daniel A. Kanipe, age twenty-three, was riding along the bluffs when the camp came into view. "We were then charging at full speed," Kanipe recalled. ". . . Reno and his troops were seen again to our left, moving at full speed down the valley. At the sight of the Indian camps, the boys of our five troops began to cheer."[14] Within a short time, however, every cheering voice would be stilled forever. Luckily for Sergeant Kanipe, Tom Custer had dispatched him to the rear to inform McDougall and the pack train to hurry up, and if possible, to tell Benteen to hurry as well. At about this same time, Benteen decided that if he was going to be of any assistance to the command, he would need to join them as quickly as possible. He believed—quite correctly—that his jaunt was a useless adventure, and that only his decision to disobey orders now would put him in a position to help the command once contact with the hostiles was actually made. Little did Benteen realize that this "disobedience" would result in the salvation of Reno's bloodied command. As Sergeant Kanipe galloped away, he heard Custer call out, "Hold your horses in, boys, there are plenty of them down there for us all."[15]

Private William O. Taylor took part in that momentous charge into the valley. Writing about it years later, Taylor said that as the Indians came into view, they could see activity in the camp. "[W]e were then at a fast walk. Then as little puffs of smoke were seen and the 'ping' of bullets spoke out plainly, we were ordered to charge."[16] As soon as the troops started to charge, they, like their doomed counterparts on the bluffs, began to cheer. But this obviously irritated Reno, who immediately called out "Stop that noise!" "As I looked back," Taylor added, "Major Reno was just taking a bottle from his lips. He then passed it to Lieutenant Hodgson. It appeared to be a quart flask, about one-half to two-thirds full. . . ."[17]

First Sergeant John M. Ryan of Company M remembered well the charge onto the wide and open valley on that hot Sunday afternoon.

He recalled that while they were galloping, Lieutenant Charles Varnum called out, "[T]hirty days' furlough to the man who gets the first scalp!"[18] Although Ryan was eager for a furlough, he didn't share Varnum's enthusiasm for a scalp. Given the fact that Varnum had seen a portion of the Indian village just a short time earlier, and had come to the conclusion that the camp contained an "immense number of Indians . . . more than I ever saw before,"[19] one has to wonder whether his statement about the scalp contained more gallows humor than sincerity.

Meanwhile, the Sioux and Cheyenne took action to save their people. Riding their ponies back and forth, the warriors created clouds of dust that served as a smoke screen while the women, children, and elderly had time to escape. Years later, Chief Gall of the Hunkpapa Sioux remembered how rapidly Reno had swept down into the valley, forcing the warriors into a premature fight.[20] Of course, Reno's trek into the valley put him on a collision course with the large camp. Besides the dust billowing up before them, which served the Indians well, the warriors had also started a number of fires on the dry prairie. Up till now, the Sioux had kept themselves just outside rifle range, acting as a buffer between the camp and the soldiers. Yet this charge, which was destined to become an important part of the legacy of Marcus A. Reno, came skidding to an abrupt halt. From this moment on, confusion would reign within the ranks of the Seventh Cavalry.

Although the valley appeared flat—with the Little Bighorn River snaking its way on the troopers' right, and with foothills on the left—Reno testified that he saw a ditch containing a large number of Indians, who came pouring out onto the plain. This fact was confirmed by several other officers, including Lieutenant Wallace. Reno aborted the charge at a place where the river looped out leftward onto the prairie. Directly in front of this loop was a timber of young cottonwood trees that contained a glade, or swale, in its center. Just as the troopers approached this timber, some of the men fired their weapons into the woods so that any Indians hiding there would be encouraged to leave.[21] Two unfortunate souls who were unable to control their horses continued galloping toward the village and were swallowed up by the enraged Sioux. As the skirmish line was formed, the right end of the line reached the timber and continued leftward out toward the foothills. This is where scouts George Herendeen and Charley Reynolds, along with interpreter Fred Girard, had positioned themselves to keep out of the soldiers' way.

The Sioux, whose actions up until now had remained defensive, would soon press the attack, and Reno would not have to wait very long. Having dismounted, the troops began a concentrated fire at the Indians, who were still some five to eight hundred yards away. Although the firing at this distance was not accurate, the .45 caliber carbine rounds did begin falling into camp, puncturing tepees, hitting ponies, and wounding and killing a number of the Sioux and Cheyenne. In a July 1886 interview that appeared in the *St. Paul Pioneer Press*, Chief Gall related how he was transformed through his own personal loss as Reno's skirmish line fired into the village: "My two squaws and three children were killed there . . . and it made my heart bad. After that I killed all my enemies with the hatchet."[22] According to Sergeant Ryan, the first to fall dead on the line that day was Sergeant Miles F. O'Hara, of Company M. A corporal just days before, O'Hara had been promoted to sergeant because Sergeant Dolan's military term of service was about to expire. Dolan missed the battle, as he was allowed to remain at the base camp at Powder River.

Many of the troops were very green and inexperienced, and were firing their weapons rapidly, despite the protests of the officers. Testifying later, Myles Moylan said that it was "impossible for an officer to regulate it, owing to the men being new in the service, and not under fire before."[23] Sergeant Edward Davern was situated to the left of the line, and had crawled about two hundred yards ahead of the firing line to shoot at some Indians another two hundred yards farther out. He also took notice of the rapid firing. Still situated to the left of the line were scouts Herendeen, Reynolds, and Girard. As they sat there watching the troops hurling lead at the distant village, they decided to set the sights of their rifles on one particular Indian. The distance, however, was too great, and as Herendeen remembered it, "We could see all the balls fall short of the Indian."[24]

It must be noted that the officers' testimony varied regarding the number of Indians they were facing. However, it does seem certain that within minutes of the skirmish line being formed, there were several hundred yelping warriors facing them, and that their numbers were gaining in strength by the minute. Lieutenant Wallace must have felt they were quite strong, as he later testified that the Indians "were ready to receive us."[25] It wasn't long before the soldiers' entire front was blanketed with warriors who were doing an excellent job of flanking the troops and forcing the left wing to give ground. Although the line endeavored to maintain its position, the left end was forced to bend back and soon would be almost parallel to the river. At about this same time, Reno led Company G through the timber to a spot where a few Indian lodges from the southernmost tip of the camp nearly touched the woods. Evidently, he was concerned about a hostile infiltration from that direction and was attempting to avert any problems that would come from a breach in the line. While a breach in his line was not yet a reality, a breach in his mind was about to occur.

As Reno made his way through the woods with G Company, he was fully aware of the deteriorating situation of the skirmish line, and it only stands to reason that Custer's "no-show" was playing on his mind as well. According to Lieutenant Wallace, twenty of those following Reno were new recruits to G Company, having been picked up by the regiment in April in St. Paul, Minnesota. One can easily imagine their state of mind as, unfamiliar carbines in hand, they followed their wide-eyed leader through the woods to God only knew where, all the while silent regrets poured out of them as forcefully as the sweat that was now drenching their clothes.

Meanwhile, the warriors were vigorously pressing the attack, and the withdrawal of G Company from the line for Reno's trek through the timber did not help matters at all. Unable to hold the line any longer, the troops headed for the woods. Lieutenant Varnum said that while the timber was quite thick, there were paths leading into it made by the various animals inhabiting the area. Even so, their time spent in the woods would be very short. Indeed, the confusion which drove the troops from the prairie only followed them into the trees. The blue-coated hunters had now become the blue-coated hunted. The warriors, spurred on by their successful intimidation of the soldiers, now swirled around the timber, shouting and firing into it at will. For some of the troops, being driven into the woods did have its advantages, as a number of them were out of ammunition and could at least now get to their horses and retrieve more.

As can be expected of those who feel that momentum is going their way, the Indians were becoming bolder in their actions, breaching the lines in several places, and soon a steady rain of bullets was falling on the men. As Reno discussed the situation with several officers, he came to the conclusion that the command should make a run for the hills on the other side of the Little Bighorn River. Although Reno almost imme-diately began calling this action a "charge," he did refer to it once as a "retreat" when discussing the situation with Captain Moylan.

As Reno conferred with the scout Bloody Knife concerning the pos-sible intention of the hostiles, several bullets streaked into their midst, killing Bloody Knife and a Private Lorentz. Bloody Knife, who was standing just several feet away from Reno, was hit in the head, the impact of which showered the major with the blood and brains of the dead scout. During the Civil War, Reno had seen plenty of head wounds, and blood spewing like geysers from the bodies of those mortally wounded was cer-tainly nothing new to him. Still, the incident does appear to be the pro-verbial straw that broke the camel's back. Having succumbed to at least some degree of terror, the major bolted from the timber, followed by those lucky enough to have heard the order to retreat. Before leaving the woods, however, Reno was so completely flustered by the killing of Bloody Knife and Private Lorentz that he ordered those around him to dismount, but just as quickly changed his mind and ordered them to mount up again. Thoughts of personal disaster must have been racing through his mind faster than the bullets that were zipping past his ears. Within seconds, Reno was bounding out of the woods.

As commanding officer, Reno could have banished such confusion among his troops by employing the proper bugle calls and should have done so. The blaring sound of a bugle would have certainly stood out among the shrieks of the Indians, the cussing of the troops, and the blasts of rifles, which by now had become quite steady. Given the stark facts of this exodus, it is very difficult to view Reno's flight from the woods as anything but an attempt at self-preservation. Herendeen believed that the killing of Bloody Knife startled everyone and was to blame for the quick departure. At about the same time this was occurring, Lieutenant Varnum began to notice that "a great many bullets had commenced to drop into the woods from our rear. . . . I could hear the bullets chip the trees as they would strike."[26] Lieutenant Hare, who later testified that he was unaware that an order to leave the timber had been given, said that he first learned of the move when Private Clare of K Company brought him his horse. Had it not been for Private Clare, Lieutenant Hare believed, he might have been left to his fate in the woods. Sadly, Clare, whose hands brought deliverance to the lieutenant, would not be counted among the survivors at battle's end.

Dr. Henry Porter, the only physician of three to survive the expedition, remembered hearing someone saying, "We had to get out of here, that we had to charge the Indians."[27] But the good doctor was of the opinion that instead of the troops charging the Indians, it appeared the Indians were driving the troops, adding, "Every man seemed to be running on his own hook." Girard said the troops were in a great hurry to get out, and that "there seemed to be no order at all. Every man was for himself."[28] As they rode off, Girard said he heard an officer shout out: "For God's sake men—don't leave—we have wounded."[29] Herendeen later would identify this officer as Lieutenant Charles Varnum, but Varnum's cries went unheeded.

The distance between the timber and where the command would cross the Little Bighorn River (the troops were actually forced to retreat in a southeasterly direction, rather than in a straight line) was between one-half and three-quarters of a mile away, and the Indians, already surrounding the cavalrymen in great numbers, were determined to kill as many of them as they could before they had a chance to cross the river.

As Reno "led" the command across the prairie toward the river, the fighting was desperate. Sergeant Ryan remembered, "As we cut through them the fighting was hand to hand, and it was death to any man who fell from his horse."[30] Many warriors were content to gallop alongside the soldiers, picking them off with steady fire from their weapons. Lieutenant Varnum recalled how the Indians would "sit there and work their rifles."[31] For these warriors, using the latest repeating rifles, it must have seemed more like a buffalo hunt than a contest of equals. The soldiers, who offered absolutely no organized response to this enfilading fire, would suffer heavy casualties in what can only be considered a gauntlet-like retreat. Unknown to Reno's men, a number of the Sioux chasing them were not just shouting their war cry, but were chiding them because they mistakenly believed they had whipped them along the Rosebud, an obvious reference to General Crook's defeat eight days earlier.[32]

As the troops plunged their horses down the embankment and into the water, Reno paused to survey the scene. The rear of the column was now swirling in confusion as the Indians kept up a steady fire into what Reno could only describe as "a very large target."[33] Dr. Porter remembered that he had quite a bit of difficulty mounting his horse when it came time to leave the woods. After dashing through a group of warriors who were between him and the command, as well as a large number who were to his right, firing into the troops, he neared the riverbank. Like Reno, Porter could see that the rear of the command was "in no order at all. Every man seemed to be running on his own hook."[34] He could also see warriors on the other side of the river, firing down at a dozen or so troops who were still in the water. At no time did he see any officer attempting to stabilize the situation, adding that he saw no officers at all until he crossed the river. At least one officer did attempt to stem the tide of confusion. The scout Herendeen, who later said the troops were running for their lives, remembered one officer shouting, "Company A men, halt . . . let us fight them; for God's sake, don't run."[35] This officer was probably Lieutenant Varnum.

The hilltop the troops were trying so desperately to reach was extremely steep and accessible by various jagged ravines and gullies, which led up to the top. Unfortunately, some of these ravines were accessible to the Indians as well, either in person or well within the sights of their rifles. Doctor DeWolf, having survived the perilous flight from the timber, was cut down in one of these gullies by Indians firing down from the hilltop. Varnum, following behind DeWolf, was warned just in time by the shouts of the others who had seen the hostiles positioning themselves, thereby escaping the same fate of the fallen doctor. Many of the men led their horses up these ravines, although more than a few remained mounted as they ascended the hill. Indeed, some wounded troopers made it all the way to the top before sliding or falling off their mounts. Evidently, in the midst of the chaos, one trooper decided to take Lieutenant Varnum at his word, for he was seen ascending the hill with the scalp of a Sioux clutched in his hand.

In terms of casualties, the race from the timber was very costly: over thirty dead, and half a dozen wounded. True to his inner feeling, Charley Reynolds was among the dead who fell in the valley fight. Witnesses said the Indians shot his horse out from under him; the horse then fell on Reynolds, pinning him under its weight. After the fight, those who had the opportunity of reclaiming the dead said he had put up a good fight, as a number of empty cartridge cases were scattered around him.

It was between 3:30 and 4:00 p.m. when Benteen's troop approached the scene of Reno's fiasco. After fording the Little Bighorn, Benteen followed Custer's route and headed up the bluffs, for he had seen Reno's men being driven off the skirmish line and into the timber. At this time Benteen was not aware that the confused fight did not include the entire regiment. Benteen's arrival on the hilltop, as well as the arrival of the pack train an hour later, would be a critical factor in the salvation of Reno's shaken band. Salvation for Custer, however, was now beyond the realm of possibility, as events were unfolding very quickly. Nothing would deter Custer from obtaining a great victory over the Sioux.

CHAPTER 11

Field of Death

After watching the opening of Reno's attack from the bluffs, Custer rode on with his five jubilant companies over the high ground, never to be seen again. Yet even having the advantage of being in an elevated position, he was yet to learn the true size of the militant Indian encampment. The horses, already suffering exhaustion from the pace of the preceding days, labored heavily under this gallop of death. In Custer's mind, however, everything was falling into place: He finally had the enemy right where he wanted them. The decisive blow against the rebellious Sioux and Cheyenne was about to be struck, and he was happy to be playing a very important part in their defeat. He was also fully aware that people back east would soon be reading of his exploits in the wilds of Montana. He knew that a victory over the Plains Indians would work in his favor as he pursued other ventures once his military career came to an end.

As they raced northward, an even clearer view of the camp appeared, and it was evidently here that Custer dispatched his first messenger to the rear (Sergeant Daniel Kanipe), to gather the command that he himself had dispersed. It was at this time that Custer traveled down a narrow ravine that would, after about one mile, lead into a coulee named the Medicine Tail. At about the same time, Custer decided to send a second courier to the rear. It is clear from these actions that second thoughts were starting to take hold in his mind. He was wondering how far the pack train was from them, and he was considering the useless jaunt he now understood Benteen was conducting. Even so, he still had time to turn things around and give way to caution by either halting where he was or marching to the rear until he had joined with the others. But that was not to be, as something continued to drive him in the direction of destruction. This pivotal moment, when he could have saved himself and the five companies moving ahead with him, was lost.

In any event, Custer called out to trumpeter Martini, ordering him to ride back and intercept Captain Benteen, instructing him to hurry up the pack train. Just as Martini was about to pull the reins on his horse to turn around, Lieutenant W. W. Cooke arrived. He hurriedly scribbled out a note, and, ripping the page from his small notebook, handed it to the last white man who would ever see Custer's command alive:

> *Benteen.*
> *Come on. Big village.*
> *Be quick. Bring packs.*
> *W. W. Cooke*
> *P.S. Bring pack [sic]*

Martini dug his spurs into his horse and galloped away. Within seconds of this he heard gunfire, and, turning around in his saddle, saw Indians firing at the troopers and waving blankets to startle their horses. After riding full speed for a short distance, he slowed up at the sight of Boston Custer riding toward him at a full gallop. Boston was trying to catch up with his brother before the attack commenced. "He was running hard," Martini remembered, "but when he saw me he checked his horse and shouted 'Where's the General?' And I answered, 'Right behind the next ridge you'll find him.'"[1] And he did.

As Martini rode back along the bluffs, he looked to his right and saw Reno's men in action on the skirmish line, which had already begun to give ground under Sioux pressure. Just then, Indians spotted him above them and started firing their rifles. Martini was aware of this but was not hit by any of the bullets. As his mount continued to carry him without any signs that anything was wrong, he assumed the horse had escaped unharmed—that is, until Benteen pointed out a stream of blood coming from his horse. Martini was an exceedingly lucky man that day.

Benteen, after disobeying Custer's order to continue on, finally linked up with the main trail just a short distance from the Lone Warrior tepee, which was now burning. According to Benteen, it was here that Custer's first messenger came into view. Sergeant Kanipe quickly relayed the message that he'd received from Captain Tom Custer, to "hurry up the packs."[2] Benteen sent him on to the pack train, which, unbeknownst to Benteen, was only one mile in the rear. Accompanied by his orderly, Benteen rode four or five hundred yards in advance of his battalion. When he encountered Martini and read the note, he ordered the command to proceed at a trot. Galloping ahead, he reached the Little Bighorn before the rest of the command. He could see Reno's men being "thrashed" in the valley, but he was at that time unaware that it was only Reno's men and not the entire command. Martini, not realizing the desperate situation Custer was now in, told Benteen that the Indians were "skedaddling," but, Benteen said, "My first sight of the fight showed that there was no skedaddling being done."[3]

Within minutes Benteen's troops were charging up the bluffs, pistols drawn, fully expecting to meet the Sioux once the top was reached. But instead of painted faces and feathered heads, they found the hilltop swarming with Reno's beaten remnant. It was now approaching 4:00 p.m. But where was Custer? It is important to note that once Martini had ridden away from Custer, it is impossible to ascertain what exactly occurred with Custer's doomed contingent. Indian testimony varies and is sometimes conflicting in nature, and because no white men lived to tell the tale, it is difficult to interpret the exact sequence of events. Now that all participants are long dead, some events will forever remain shrouded in mystery. Archaeology—that "voice" from the ground—has unearthed some interesting facts concerning the battle, yet even the slow, methodical hand of the archaeologist cannot tell us everything.

A word about Indian testimony is important as well. Unlike soldiers, who are ordered into battle by their officers and must remain with their respective units, the warrior is free to choose his own course in battle. If he desires to be part of a particular attacking group, he is free to join them.

If not, he's free to fight however he wishes. For example, when Crazy Horse became aware of Reno's valley attack, he shouted out for the brave ones to follow him while ordering cowards to the rear. Of course, a man like Crazy Horse inspired those around him by his actions, as did other Indians who were recognized as leaders. Although warriors were known to move as "units," the participants were free to leave at any time and scurry around the battlefield however they pleased.

During the chaotic Custer fight, the warriors joined the battle at different times and at various places, and as the tide of battle carried people over the hills and gullies so prevalent in this area of the country, each Indian would later carry his own mental picture of how events had unfolded. This is quite natural, and confusion concerning certain aspects can occur. In addition, it must be remembered that all Indian testimony came after—sometimes years after—the fight occurred, and the speaker was now a "conquered" Indian living in a dominant white culture. As such, the Indians may have been more likely to relay certain events in a manner that would please their white audience rather than to tell the truth. After all, some of these veterans took on almost celebrity status and became very adept at raking in the white man's coin. Why should they depress their audience by telling them the truth when they could sugarcoat it, keep them happy, and make a living for themselves as well?

In any case, after dispatching Martini, Custer rode down Medicine Tail Coulee, but just how far is open to question. It is certain that perhaps two companies did reach the river's edge, as artifacts such as US Army carbine shell casings have been found at this spot.[4] This supports some Indian testimony that stated the soldiers came to the river's edge and fired across the river at the camp. These troops, comprising the left wing, would soon move northward and away from the river in their attempt to rejoin the main command, which had been deployed on the high ground known today as the Nye-Cartwright Ridge.

Although it is now a point of controversy, Custer probably did not encounter a horde of Indians at this location, although there were warriors making themselves targets. Even so, their numbers did grow rapidly, and Chief Gall would soon cross the river and attack the troops who were now falling back. By this time, Custer's five companies were well on their way to their final destination. Although the command was still functioning as an organized unit, it would not be long before small pockets of disintegration would appear as the Seventh Cavalry moved across the valleys and hills like a snake seeking refuge.

After the bulk of Reno's men had reached the hilltop, they began noticing that many of the Indians had begun racing back through the village, going in the direction of where they must have believed Custer had gone. This abrupt move by the Indians would give Reno's troops time to recover and prepare a defense. This release of warriors would also help turn the tide against Custer. The very thing Benteen had warned him about was now taking place. And so, as the full force of Indians began to concentrate their efforts on the five companies, they would employ a tactic of infiltration which would prove very effective. The ground over which the soldiers were forced to fight is marked by hills, gullies, and ravines, and as the battle developed, the troops began to fall over a wide area of this rough ground.

When exactly Custer began to see his situation as serious remains a mystery, but there is no question that, as the strength of the hostiles became apparent and the reinforcements from Benteen and Reno did not arrive, the question of survival must have become very real to him. Did he at this time remember the warning of his scouts or the conversation with Benteen? Although we will never know, it seems likely. What we do know is that as the soldiers swarmed up and down the various gullies and hills, they exchanged fire with the Indians. Most of the warriors were wisely fighting on foot, using the ground to their advantage. Although this infiltration would take some time, and would consist of Indian movements both north of Custer and south of the command; once the battle began in earnest, the destruction of the five companies would come very quickly. The Indians had not had it so good—or so easy—since the fight with the arrogant Captain Fetterman on that frigid December day almost ten years earlier. Today, however, the blue-coats were fighting under a blistering sun, their clothes drenched with sweat, the steel portion of their weapons hot to the touch.

Years of frustration were boiling over in the hearts and minds of the Sioux and Cheyenne warriors. This day would see leaders such as the famed Crazy Horse, Gall, Rain-in-the-Face, and others overwhelming and annihilating the elite Seventh Cavalry, and they would do so with a speed and determination that would make any West Point instructor proud. As the troops gave ground under pressure, some groups proved to be more orderly than others. However, when panic ensued, disintegration followed by death came very quickly. After Lieutenant Calhoun's position was overrun, the remnants fled northward into Captain Keogh's Company I. But a mounted attack by Crazy Horse's warriors brought destruction on most of these as well. Soon all of the groups were killed, leaving Custer's huddled mass to deal with.

The smoke and dust of battle, the screams of the wounded, and the sound of eagle-bone whistles filled the air. As the fight continued to the spot known today as Last Stand Hill, the officers and men shot their horses, instantly transforming the animals into protective breastworks. The hostiles, firing various weapons and hurling arrows with metal heads, would engulf the boy general and all those who looked to him for deliverance. But there would be no deliverance on this day, and an unlikely epitaph was about to be written. When Custer fell, it was directly across from the camp of the Cheyenne, and what had been promised to him as he sat under the medicine arrows had now come to pass. In this sense, his death became terribly ironic, something in which the Cheyenne took great pleasure.

The spot where George Armstrong Custer fell is just short of the summit where the monument now stands. It is almost certain that Custer had intended to reach this summit but was prevented from doing so. Perhaps reaching the top would have given Custer a little more time, but that time could be calculated in minutes only and would have made absolutely no difference in the final outcome. Just as he would not help Reno, Reno could not help him. When found, Custer was lying in a semi-propped-up position between two other corpses. Witnesses said that he looked very calm, which is not surprising. He had two bullet wounds, one in the left chest, and one near his left temple, although the head wound was undoubtedly postmortem.

But how and when did Custer die? There are numerous accounts of how he died, and all of them come from the ones who destroyed the Seventh Cavalry on June 25, 1876. The Indians were unaware at the time just who it was they were killing, but once it was discovered they had defeated "Long Hair," it became fashionable to take credit for his death. In truth, it is impossible to ascertain today exactly who felled this famous military icon. Two months before his death, Rain-in-the-Face, who hated Tom Custer because he had once arrested him, made what I believe to be a fair assessment of the nature and the ferocity of this battle when he said: "In that fight the excitement was so great that we scarcely recognized our nearest friends."[5] One version of Custer's death came down from Chief Sitting Bull and was published in the *New York Herald* in 1877. This story, apparently given by warriors returning from the fight, is certain to please white ears. According to this account, Custer, at battle's end, was one of just several soldiers left alive, laughing and killing an Indian as he fell. To be sure, if this is how it happened, it was a gallant death for Custer, and it makes for good reading. But I believe that Sitting Bull's version of his death is little more than fiction.

One scenario which does at least seem plausible is that Custer was shot by a young Oglala by the name of Joseph White Crow Bull as he journeyed down Medicine Tail Coulee. What gives this incident the ring of truth is that the man Joseph shot was wearing buckskin (Custer was wearing buckskin trousers that morning), and he was riding next to a flag-bearing soldier. Perhaps most importantly, after this man was shot, a good many troopers were seen closing up around him.[6] If this report is indeed accurate, then Custer was felled, if not killed, early in the engagement. One can easily imagine the confusion which must have swirled in the minds of those who witnessed Custer's death, the general tumbling from his saddle like a mere mortal. This was unthinkable, a terrible reality come to life. Whether he made his way up to the ridge to Last Stand Hill under his own power or was borne up by his faithful subordinates will forever remain within the realm of speculation, as will so many other aspects of this quick and decisive battle. Yet if he were mortally wounded at Medicine Tail Coulee, this could explain why so many officers died with Custer instead of with their respective companies.

However death came to George Armstrong Custer, it is certain that he died as he had lived: a soldier. I'm convinced that as he saw the situation deteriorating, he faced it with a calm resolve, determined to hold out to the end, and true to his character, taking as many of his adversaries with him as possible. On more than one occasion during the Civil War, Custer wrote to Libbie, telling her that even during the heat of battle, when shot and shell were whirling past his head, he was thinking of her.[7] Perhaps it was being so close to extinction that caused him to dwell with her mentally at such times. Whatever it was, when his life started slipping away and he realized that all was lost, it must have been thoughts of Libbie that burned in his mind during those final moments. The famous military icon was paying the price he had caused so many others to pay, on so many battlefields before, and he knew it.

Unlike many of the troopers who died that day, Custer was not mutilated by the Indians. However, according to Indian tradition, two Cheyenne women recognized Custer and used sewing awls to puncture his eardrums so that in the afterlife he might hear better than he had while on Earth. They were, of course, remembering the 1869 warning he had received while sitting under the medicine arrows, and his promise to never again make war with the Cheyenne people.

The task of burying the dead fell to the survivors of Reno's hilltop siege. Because of the hard soil and the shortage of shovels, most of the enlisted men were interred under only a few inches of earth. Custer and the officers received a deeper and more-thorough burial, and also had rocks placed over their graves. All were buried at the places on the field where they had fallen. Within a year, the army ordered that the officers' remains be disinterred and brought back east for formal burials by their families. The enlisted men were buried in a mass grave on Last Stand Hill.

What of Indian casualties? Estimates of Indian dead for the Custer battle run as high as one hundred and as low as forty. Whatever their true number, all had been removed from the field by the time that General Terry's column arrived at the site on June 27.

As was their custom, the Sioux left their dead in lodges or on scaffolds. The Cheyenne would place their fallen within the sides of cliffs or in rock crevices. A trooper visiting the field in 1877 told of walking among the bones of the Sioux which had fallen through the scaffold. In one of the skulls he spotted a bullet, no doubt fired from one of the dead men occupying Custer Hill. According to Chief Gall, the wounded of the battle fared little better than those killed instantly, with as many dying each day as were killed during the battle. Within the hearts and minds of both cultures, the valley of the Little Bighorn would never be the same.

After annihilating Custer and his five companies, the Indians began concentrating their efforts on those gathered at the spot known today as Reno Hill. Thoroughly energized by their decisive win on Last Stand Hill, they expected to complete the slaughter with Reno and Benteen as well. But here, events would not unfold for the Sioux and Cheyenne as they anticipated. Soon after the Indians began leaving the Reno position to join the fight against the five companies, who were even then being dispersed, much firing was heard downstream. Some said they could hear volley firing, while others said the firing was more general. If it was volley firing (and most likely it was), then it was an attempt by Custer to draw attention to his plight. One can easily imagine him barking out orders to fire, say, at the count of three. But the unified crack of the Springfield model 1873 carbine would go unanswered. In any event, whatever type of shooting was echoing throughout the valley, most believed it involved Custer. Lieutenant Varnum remarked that a few minutes after Benteen arrived on the hill, he also heard firing, but that it sounded like "a heavy fire—a sort of crash, crash," adding that he thought Custer was having a "warm time" down there.[8] Even so, the idea that Custer could be wiped out never entered his mind. It was unthinkable.

While Varnum was obviously maintaining a positive attitude about things, demoralization and the sense of being whipped certainly were becoming a problem for a number of officers and enlisted men alike. Of course, no one likes to admit demoralization, especially military people, and so as time elapsed, certain individuals attempted to put a better face on the situation where possible. One of these was Lieutenant Hare, yet Lieutenant Godfrey remembers Hare meeting him atop Reno Hill, shaking his hand and exclaiming, "We've had a big fight in the valley, got whipped like hell and I'm damned glad to see you."[9] Upon reaching the top of the hill, Reno was seen blazing away with his pistol at the Indians who were now about a thousand yards away. This must have been from utter frustration, as Reno knew the effective range of his Colt army-issue pistol did not exceed one hundred yards. Benteen, who would later take great pains to avoid using the word "demoralized" when testifying before the Reno Court of Inquiry, did admit years later in personal correspondence with an ex-Seventh Cavalry trooper just how bad a time certain officers were having. According to Benteen, his first sight upon reaching the top of the hill was of Captain Myles Moylan, who was "blubbering like a whipped urchin, tears coursing down his cheeks."[10]

Using a carbine, but like Reno, also out of range, Varnum was firing at the retreating hostiles. Some have said he was crying as well. The flight from the valley had been an undeniably emotional one, whose cost in dead and wounded could have been greatly reduced had Reno exercised proper leadership, beginning with ordering the proper bugle calls to be sounded while still in the timber.

Before the pack train had even arrived, Captain Thomas Weir took an unauthorized ride to a high point a little over one mile north of their present position. Benteen would later refer to Weir's northern rise as "a fit of bravado."[11] Soon Lieutenant Edgerly came galloping up with Troop D, and a short time later, by other elements of the command, the idea being to open up communication with Custer. In the distance they could see a great deal of dust and activity in what turned out to be the Custer battlefield. However, by this time, the battle was well over; the only movements now occurring were the mutilating and looting of the command. But the Seventh's foray northward would be short-lived, as the Sioux and Cheyenne, drunk with victory, came calling again on those occupying Reno Hill.

The hilltop that now became the focal point of the battle was described by Lieutenant Varnum as being "rather rough. That is, the top was uneven and rolling."[12] This irregular hilltop would in some ways prove to be beneficial to the Indians as they crept forward to fire at the troops. But that same aspect was greatly helpful to the soldiers, too; the circular depression that can still be seen today was used by Dr. Porter to work on and care for the wounded. Indeed, most of the land appears today as it was back in 1876, except for the Little Bighorn River, whose snakelike course has changed somewhat over the years.

Private Charles Windolph said that the men had barely reached their positions back on the bluffs when the Indians, having surrounded them, began pressing the attack.[13] Over the next three hours, the Seventh would suffer an additional eighteen men killed and forty-six wounded.[14] When the sun finally set on the hard-pressed command, Lieutenant Wallace remembered it going down as a "red ball."[15] While some of the men on the hill feared a nighttime attack by the Sioux, none would be forthcoming. Still, sleeping would be all but impossible for some. Lieutenant Edgerly passed Reno several times on the night of June 25. "He asked me what I had been doing," Edgerly remembered. "I said that I had been asleep. He said 'Great God, I don't see how you could sleep.'"[16]

Between 2:30 and 3:00 a.m., just as daylight began stretching itself across the command, it brought with it another onslaught from the Sioux and Cheyenne warriors. According to Lieutenant Wallace, between 10:00 a.m. and noon on the 26th, the fire was particularly heavy. Some Indians mistakenly set up their positions outside the range of their guns, and the bullets from these weapons fell harmlessly among the soldiers who could then pick them up.[17] At times, the only target the troopers would have to aim at would be the puffs of smoke giving away the warriors' position. "There would be a lull," Wallace remembered, "and then it would start again, and the bullets would come in like hail."[18] The troops used a method to flush out their enemy, by refusing to return fire. After a while, the warriors became confident they had done some real damage to the soldiers and would jump up and rush toward the troops—a mistake, as they were met with a wall of spinning hot lead coming at them. But even with this steady fusillade of .45 caliber bullets, some areas were more vulnerable than others, and as a result, some companies suffered more casualties than others. At times, some warriors were so close to the soldiers they were able to throw dirt clods at the surprised troopers.

Because of this pressure, Benteen told Reno that unless something was done, the entire command could be overrun. Reno allowed Benteen to carry out his plans, and so, after assembling a group of troops together, Benteen gave the men a quick pep talk relating the problem and what he proposed to do about it. Leading the charge himself, Benteen drove the astonished Indians away, thereby eliminating a potentially disastrous problem. Although second in command on the hill, Benteen later testified, "Mind you, I was looking after things probably more than it was my business or duty to do."[19] Benteen was not alone in this assessment of Major Marcus Reno. Lieutenant Godfrey found no comfort in Reno's indecision or lack of confidence. After discussing the situation with Captain Weir, Godfrey decided that it was to "Benteen we must look for the wisdom to deliver us."[20]

Although Benteen's Company H was exposed to a withering fire, their captain exhibited an absolute calm. "Captain Benteen came over and stood near where I was on a high point." Lieutenant Edgerly recalled, "The bullets were flying very fast there and I did not see why he was not riddled. He was perfectly calm; I remember there was a smile on his face."[21] Lieutenant Wallace also saw him in a very exposed position and wondered why he wasn't shot down. After Wallace warned him to take cover, Benteen said "something about the bullet not having been molded yet to shoot him."[22]

And while Reno failed to impress most people with his leadership while on the hill, it is quite clear he at least managed to keep his head during the siege. Far more damning than his lack of action was his discussion with Benteen that the command should abandon the wounded and make their escape the night of June 25—something Benteen would never agree to. "I killed that proposition in the bud," he later wrote.[23] Benteen later related this cowardly and un-officer-like incident to a former Seventh Cavalry trooper with whom he had been corresponding, yet he chose not to reveal it at the inquiry, the reasons for which remain a mystery today. Perhaps he felt Reno had suffered enough. Far more likely, however, was his desire to protect the reputation of the regiment. In any case, official ears would never hear of Reno's plan to abandon the wounded, and the character of the major would be the better for it.

By late afternoon on June 26, the great Indian camp had begun to depart, to the joy of the shattered troops they were leaving behind. Years later, certain Indians would make the absurd claim that the reason for their departure was that the soldiers had learned their lesson, and there was no reason for further bloodshed. This again was the voice of the conquered Indian attempting to soothe white ears. In reality, the Sioux and Cheyenne had seen the approach of the Terry-Gibbon column, and it wasn't white survival that suddenly concerned them, but their own. It was time to head for safer ground.

As news of the disaster reached the white world, a sense of shock and disbelief began to engulf the nation. The death of so many soldiers, including that of General Custer, caused much grief and amazement for the living. After General Sherman received word in Philadelphia, a reporter pressed him for a response. "I don't believe it," he said, "and I don't want to believe it if I can help it."[24] In Washington, D.C., the War Department was kept busy as the families and friends of those in Indian country sought news of their loved ones' fate.[25] From Salt Lake City newspapers came the report: "The citizens are excited over the Custer massacre." The report went on to offer the citizens' services should a "regiment of fron-tiersmen" be needed. Twenty-four hours later, the people of Salt Lake City held a meeting and resolved to raise twelve hundred men over the next ten days to avenge the death of Custer, and "for the extermination of the Sioux Indians."[26]

Even former enemies came to the aid of the fallen military icon. Former Confederate general Joe O. Shelby sent a telegram to President Ulysses S. Grant on July 7, which read: "General Custer has been killed; we once fought him and now propose to avenge him. Should you deter-mine to call volunteers, allow Missouri to raise one thousand."[27] July 7 also saw a Senator Paddoc introduce a bill that would, if President Grant "deem[ed] it necessary . . . accept the service of volunteers from the state of Nebraska, and the territories of Wyoming, Colorado, Dakota, and Utah."[28] As might be expected, Monroe, Michigan, was devastated by the loss of its favorite son. By July 14, the townspeople, ever faithful to the general, took the first steps toward erecting a monument to honor the memory of the dashing young cavalryman.

The loss to the Custer family was severe indeed. Killed along with the general was his brother and close confidant in the Seventh, Tom Custer. Their younger brother, Boston, who had been serving in the regiment as a forager, also perished within feet of his famous brothers. The young Arthur Reed, nephew of the general, died, as did Lieutenant James Cal-houn, brother-in-law to the Custer clan.

Despite the calls for revenge and annihilation, it would take another fourteen years before the final curtain would fall on the Indians' way of life, at Wounded Knee in December of 1890. Like an unrelenting disease, the wheels of subjugation had been grinding away within this land for over four centuries. Wounded Knee would put an end to the possibility of any real Indian resistance. Not a pretty legacy, to be sure, yet it is often the only epitaph that can be written over those who break treaties and deal underhandedly with those in weaker positions than themselves. The Indian "problem" was finally over, and in time, the world would look away.

On the morning of July 8, 1876, people across the country were able to read the first official list of the dead and wounded. What follows is the article from the *Bismarck Tribune Extra*:

BISMARCK. JULY 8.—The *Bismarck Tribune Extra* gives the following official list of the killed and wounded in the recent encounter with the Indians on the Little Bighorn River:

Field, Staff, and Noncommissioned Staff

G. A. Custer—Brevet Major General.

W. W. Cooke—Brevet Lieutenant.

Colonel Lord—Assistant Surgeon.

J. M. DeWolf—Acting Assistant Surgeon.

W. H. Sharrow—Sergeant Major.

Henry Vose—Chief Trumpeter.

Company A

Corporals Dollans and King; Privates Armstrong, Drinan, Moody, Rawlins, McDonald, Sullivan, and Switzer.

Company B

Colonel T. W. Custer; Lieutenant H. M. Harrington; First Sergeant Bates; Sergeant Farley; Corporals French, Foley, and Ryan; Privates Allen, Brindle, King, Bucknall, Cissman, Engre, Brightfield, Fahold, Griffin, Hornet, Hattisdal, King, South, Lewis, Mayor, Phillips, Russel, Rex, Ranter, Short, Shea, Shode, Stuart, St. John, Shodied, Stanellan, Warren, Wyndom, and Wright.

Company D

Corporal Vincent Farrier; Privates Patrick Golden and Edward Hanson.

Company E

Captain A. E. Smith; Lieutenant Sturgis; First Sergeant Hohmeyer; Sergeants Egden and James; Corporal Hogan; and Privates Miller, Tweed, Noller, Cashan, Keifer, Andrews, Cresfield, Harrington, Hengge, Cavanaugh, Labaring, Mahoney, Schmidt, Lemon, Sewanson, Riebold, O'Connell, Butler, Warren, Harrison, Gilbert, Ziller, Walsh, Andrews, Assdelly, Burke, Cheever, McGue, McCarthy, Dogan, Maxwell, Scott, Babcock, Perkins, Tarbox, Dye, Tessier, Galvin, Graham, Hamilton, Snow, and Hughes.

Company K

First Sergeant Winney, Sergeant Hughes, Corporal Callahan, Trumpeter Helmer, and Private Ed St. Clair.

Company I

Colonel M. Keogh; Lieutenant J. E. Porter; First Sergeant Varden; Sergeant Bastars; Corporals Wide and Morris Staples; Interpreters J. McGracer and J. Parden; Blacksmith H. Bailey; Trumpeters McElroy and Mooney; Privates Brondeharst, Barrey, Conner, Darcy, Davis, Farrell, Hilly, Haber, Hemil, Henderson, Leddison, O'Conner, Rood, Reese, Smith, Stellar, Stafford, Schoab, Smallwood, Tarr, Vanzant, Walker, Bryen, and Knight.

Company F

Colonel G. W. Yates; Lieutenant Bulley; First Sergeant Kenny; Sergeants Mersey, Vickary, and Wilkinson; Corporals Coleman and Freeman; Farriers Braidy and Brandson; Blacksmith Fanning; Privates Atchison, Brown, Bruce, Brady, Burnes, Colter, Carney, Donan, Donelly, Gardner, Hammond, Klein, Kryarth, Human, Loose, Milton, Madison, Monroe, Ridden, Ometting, Sycfoz, Saunders, Warren, May, Levick, Kelly, Driscoll, Gillet, Gross, Holcomb, Hoen, Hittismer, Lehman, Lloyd, Macharge, Litchell, Lashally, O'Brien, Parker, Pitten, Post, Quinn, Reed, Rossburg, Tymons, Troy, Vanbramer, and Whalley.

Company G

Captain McIntosh; Sergeants Batziel and Colsedine; Corporals Martin, Hagman, and Wells; Farrier Henry Doge; Teamsters Crawford and Saddler; Privates Rogers, Monroe, McGinnis, Leballey, Stefferman, and Rupp.

Company H

Corporal Lee; Privates Jones and Meade.

Company M

Sergeant H. Harris; Corporals Sooltie and Struger; Privates Gorden, Klotzbrusher, French, Myer, Smith, Semers, Tanner, Fenley, and Voight.

Twentieth Infantry

Lieutenant John J. Crittenden.

Civilians

Boston Custer, Arthur Reed, Mark Kellogg, Charles Reynolds, and Frank C. Mann.

Indian Scouts

Bloody Knife, Bobtailed Bull, and Stab.

Recapitulation

Commissioned officers killed: 14

Acting assistant surgeons killed: 1

Enlisted men killed: 237

Civilians killed: 5

Indian scouts killed: 3

The Wounded

The following is a full list of the wounded: Privates Davis Corry, Company I, Seventh Cavalry, right hip; Patrick McDonnell, Company D, left leg; Sergeant Kohn Wahl, Company H, back; Private Michael C. Mullen, Company K, right leg; Wm. George, Company H, left side, died July 3, at 4 a.m.; First Sergeant Wm. Heyn, Company A, left knee; Private John McVay, Company C, hip; Patrick Corcoran, Company K, right shoulder; Max Wicke, Company K, left foot; Alfred Whittier, Company C, right elbow; Peter Thompson, Company C, right hand; Jacob Diehl, Company A, face; J. H. Meyer, Company M, back; Roman Butler, Company M, right shoulder; Daniel Nevel, Company M, left thigh; James Mullen, Company H, right thigh; Elijah Stroude, Company A, right leg; Sergeant Polk Carney, Company M, right hip; Private James E. Benett, Company C, body, died July 5, at 3 o'clock; Frances W. Reeves, Company A, left hand and body; James Wilber, Company M, left leg; Jasper Marshall, Company L, left foot; Sergeant James T. Riley, Company E, back and left leg; Private John T. Phillips, Company H, face and both hands; Sam. Swern, Company H, both thighs; Frank

Brun, Company M, face and left thigh; Corporal Alex B. Bishop, Company H, right arm; Fred A. Olmstead, Company A, left wrist; Sergeant Charles White, Company A, right arm; Private Thomas P. Varney, Company M, right ear; Charles Campbell, Company G, right shoulder; John McGuire, Company C, right arm; Harry Black, Company H, right hand; Daniel McWilliams, Company H, right leg; Sergeant M. Riley, Company I, Seventeenth Infantry, left off at Buford, constipation; Private David Atkinson, Company C, Seventh Cavalry, left off at Buford, constipation.

Conclusion

In any discussion concerning Custer's defeat at Little Bighorn, it is important to first acknowledge that the Indians won the battle because they did everything right. The response to the attack on their village was swift, and they pursued the soldiers without letup until all were killed or had been driven to the hill. Even so, without the direct help that they received from Custer, their victory would have been vastly different or may not have occurred at all. Like the pieces to a puzzle, Custer's mistakes fit perfectly together with the choices and movements of the Indians of that decisive day. Given these circumstances, the battle unfolded in the only way it could have. Still, certain scenarios could have evolved which might have turned the tide of battle in the Seventh's favor. In exploring these, we will not only see various roads that Custer could have taken, but we will also be able to understand why this disaster became inevitable.

First of all, had the command remained a single fighting unit during the attack, it is highly unlikely that five companies would have been destroyed to a man. True, Custer may have been killed anyway and the Seventh Cavalry would have been battered, but the Indians would have suffered high casualties as well, and they would not have had the momentum that was gained by repulsing Reno without ever coming into contact with the forces under Benteen or McDougall. The isolated Custer, even with five companies, was easy to overwhelm. This would not have been the case had the entire regiment swept into the valley completely intact. Had fate taken this direction, the Battle of Little Bighorn would have been a tremendous contest, and it's anyone's guess which side would have come out on top.

Second, had Reno continued his charge into the valley, he very well may have caused enough consternation within the camp to have aided Custer by making it possible for him to mount an attack southward toward Reno. Although this must have been Custer's plan, he forgot to inform Reno, who became seriously agitated by Custer's disappearance and failure to support him. Also, had Reno continued his attack instead of making the detour into the woods and the subsequent gallop up the bluffs, he no doubt would have suffered higher casualties because he would have had to bear the brunt of the fighting until Custer could reach him. For Reno's men, this would have been disastrous. What would have occurred once Benteen arrived on the scene? No one will ever know.

The best scenario, of course, would have been the combined attack of the forces under Custer, Terry, and Gibbon. Had this occurred, the Indians would have most certainly suffered defeat. But as is always the case in war, anything can happen. Regardless of the planning by the top brass, surprises always await those going into battle. For the United States Army, June had been a humiliating month, first with the defeat of General Crook on the 17th, followed by the Custer fiasco on the 25th. The Indians not only managed to win physically against the whites, but they were also able to triumph psychologically. Crook was so shaken by the ferocity of the Sioux attack along the Rosebud that even with the prodding of General Sheridan, he refused to move against the Indians until the second week of August.

Later on, Major Reno would be judged harshly by certain individuals for his aborted charge in the valley. In some minds, Reno was the sole cause for the Custer defeat, but in light of the previously mentioned evidence, this charge is absurd. However, as commanding officer, it was his responsibility to bring order out of chaos, something he failed to do. As the highest-ranking officer in the woods, it was his duty to see to it that the command fought its way out of the timber in an organized manner. First and foremost, he should have alerted the command as to his plans to evacuate the woods by the use of bugle calls. Such an announcement would have been heard above the din of battle and would have been responded to. Had this occurred, the command could have exited the timber as one body, with the officers directing an organized fire that would have sent the Indians reeling back, forcing them to act in a defensive manner as well. Such an action would have saved many lives.

I'm sure that during Reno's flight, the warriors could hardly believe their eyes as they sat on their ponies, pumping round after round from their Winchester rifles into the startled troopers. If blame is to be laid at Reno's feet for his conduct while in the valley, then it must be laid here. If Benteen's assertion that Reno wanted to abandon the wounded is true, then his greatest transgression occurred while on the hill, remaining hidden from the command. Although Reno would ask for and receive a court of inquiry, he would never be able to emotionally let go of that disastrous Sunday. Although officially exonerated by the court, he would never be free of those who condemned him for his actions that day. One of his harshest critics was Libbie Custer, who felt that Reno was little more than a coward. Of course, in Libbie's mind, her dead husband could do no wrong, and she would spend the rest of her life defending his actions and blaming others for her husband's defeat. This is the same type of closed-minded thinking that caused Custer to die in the first place. So much for lessons learned.

Captain Benteen, on the other hand, emerged from the debacle smelling like a rose. Although some would blame him (Libbie among them) for not hurrying toward Custer once he had received the fateful message from trumpeter Martini, it's important to remember that it was Custer who had sent Benteen on that useless gallop to the left. Having heard the dire warnings of his scouts, Benteen felt it was unwise to split the regiment, and told Custer so. Besides, once Benteen arrived on the hill, he had his hands full reorganizing Reno's troops into a fighting unit again. Their attempt to help Custer, which was initiated by Captain Weir, was soon repulsed, and from that moment on, it was a case of kill or be killed for those corralled on top of the hill. After all, Custer could take care of himself; of this, everyone was confident.

And while it is no secret that Benteen despised Custer, he was too much of a professional soldier to have knowingly abandoned him to his fate. His dislike of Custer was (in his mind) quite valid, going back many years. Custer's failure to conduct a proper search for Major Elliott and his men during the Washita Campaign only intensified Benteen's hatred for him. This was not the soldierly thing to do, and Benteen knew it. At Little Bighorn, Benteen would conduct himself in the same coolheaded fashion as he always had, and the praise that he received from fellow officers and enlisted men alike for his leadership on the hill is more than well deserved. Had Custer allowed Benteen to switch places with him on June 25, the outcome of the battle would have been very different.

In the final analysis, it appears that Custer, in his attempt to overwhelm the Sioux and Cheyenne, bit off a lot more than he could chew. In his mind, the Seventh Cavalry could not fail. Like Captain Fetterman, Custer possessed that odd and arrogant belief that Indian warriors could never be a true threat to white warriors, regardless of their numbers. Between 1861 and 1865, Custer had overcome the best the South had to offer. Why would June 25, 1876, be any different? To be sure, Custer understood that death could be waiting for him during any battle, but his entire regiment being defeated by Plains Indians? Never! Such was the thinking of this thirty-six-year-old commander of the Seventh US Cavalry. And more than anything else, it would be this pattern of thinking that would cause the Indians to conquer him so easily. Caution had been thrown to the wind by Custer, and, like the wind, the Seventh Cavalry was about to be carried away to its place in history.

One factor (previously mentioned) which supposedly played a role in the fall of Custer was the jamming of the .45 single-shot Springfield carbines that the troops carried. After walking the field in which Custer's men fell, Reno found a number of broken knife blades which had been used by the frustrated troopers to manually extract the copper cartridges after their weapons failed to extract them properly. Evidently the problem was the cartridge rim, which had a tendency to snap off after the weapon became hot from firing—even though a number of breakages were said to have occurred after only several rounds had been sent though the barrel. Reno's troops experienced some breakdowns while on the hill as well, but the problem overall seemed to be very small, so it is doubtful weapon failure contributed significantly to Custer's demise. Be that as it may, it still must have been horrible for those few on Custer Hill who did experience such jamming. Their terror can easily be imagined.

Recently, an unlikely testimony has come from the ground itself. After a grass fire swept over the battlefield in 1983, a thorough archaeological examination of the area was conducted, and it proved to be very fruitful. Backed by a team of volunteers wielding that modern-day wonder, the metal detector, the archaeologists made some startling discoveries. First, they were able to locate numerous positions used by the Indians after finding the spent casings that had come from their various weapons, as well as the soldiers' carbine bullets which impacted on those areas. Second, they were able to determine how various Indians had traveled about the field during the fight by identifying the unique pattern each individual weapon made when the firing pin struck the primer on the casing (certain marks appear as the casing is extracted).

But it wasn't just bullets and copper casings that littered the field. Tragic reminders of the fight came to light as well, including a leg bone that was still inserted within the remains of an 1872 cavalry boot, the heel and sole of the boot almost completely intact. One of the most poignant finds was a wedding ring still encircling the finger bone of a long-dead husband. When further excavations were carried out at the Reno-Benteen position in May of 1989, a volunteer by the name of Monte Kloberdanz was destined to make one of the most significant discoveries in years. After growing weary of working and finding nothing in the prescribed digging area, he decided to venture down toward the Little Bighorn River. As he was examining the area over which Reno's men had crossed the river, he spotted something sticking out from the riverbank. That something turned out to be a skull, minus the lower jawbone, and two additional bones. After forensic studies were performed, the bones were determined to be those of a white individual approximately thirty to forty years of age who had died sometime in the 1870s—more precisely, on Sunday, June 25, 1876. The skull is once again beneath the earth, but this time it's in the grounds of the National Cemetery at Little Bighorn Battlefield.

In December of 1991, the Custer Battlefield National Monument underwent a name change. Proponents of the change said America has always named its battlefields after the town or area in which the fighting occurred, which of course is true. A perfect example of this would be "Gettysburg," a town, and "Antietam," a creek. As can be expected, staunch defenders of keeping things the way they have always been, as well as those who are vocal defenders of Custer, decided this should never be. Even a descendant of Custer's threatened to remove the general's personal items from the museum if the name change went through. When I visited the site, which was renamed the Little Bighorn Battlefield National Monument on Memorial Day of 1992, they informed me that Custer's descendant had since passed away.

After resting one year upon the heights above the Little Bighorn River, Custer was returned to the place where his military career had begun—West Point. Although his death occurred only fifteen years after his graduation, Custer accomplished far more in that time than most of his peers would achieve in much longer careers. When Custer's wife, Libbie, passed away in 1933, she was placed beside her husband, whom she had managed to outlive by more than half a century.

NOTES

CHAPTER 1

1. Custer, George, *My Life on the Plains*, xiii.
2. Ibid.
3. Monaghan, *Custer: The Life of General George Armstrong Custer*, 4.
4. Custer, Elizabeth, *Tenting on the Plains*, 153–55.
5. Monaghan, *Custer*, 261.
6. Custer, E. B., *Tenting on the Plains*, 150.
7. Hofling, *Custer and the Little Big Horn*, 52.
8. Custer, E. B., *Tenting on the Plains*, 2.
9. Frost, *The Custer Album: A Pictorial Biography of George Armstrong Custer*, 19.
10. Wert, *Custer: The Controversial Life of George Armstrong Custer*, 22.
11. Hutton, *The Custer Reader*, 43.
12. Ibid.
13. Ibid., 46.
14. Ibid.

CHAPTER 2

1–2. National Park Service: Civil War Defenses of Washington (online resource).
3. McPherson, *Battle Cry of Freedom*, 336.
4. Hutton, *The Custer Reader*, 46.
5. Carroll, *Custer in the Civil War: His Unfinished Memoirs*, 101–2.
6. Ibid., 101.
7. Ibid., 109.
8. Ibid., 105.
9. Sears, *George B. McClellan: The Young Napoleon*, 3.
10. McPherson, *Battle Cry of Freedom*, 426.
11. Longstreet, *From Manassas to Appomattox*, 80.

12. Merington, *The Custer Story: The Life and Intimate Letters of General George A. Custer and His Wife Elizabeth*, 27–28.
13. Carroll, *Custer in the Civil War*, 146.
14. Ibid., 149.
15–17. Ibid., 155.
18–22. Van de Water, *Glory-Hunter: A Life of General Custer*, 42–43.
23–24. Wert, *Custer*, 59.
25. Merington, *The Custer Story*, 63.

CHAPTER 3

1. Frost, *The Custer Album*, 33.
2. Kinsley, *Custer: Favor the Bold, A Soldier's Story*, 183.
3. Urwin, *Custer Victorious: The Civil War Battles of General George Armstrong Custer*, 77–78.
4. Merington, *The Custer Story*, 105.
5. Ibid.
6. Ibid., 104.
7–8. Ibid., 105.
9. Ibid., 95.
10. Ibid., 122.
11. Longstreet, *From Manassas to Appomattox*, 627.
12. Merington, *The Custer Story*, 159.
13. Custer, E. B., *Tenting on the Plains*, 1–2.

CHAPTER 4

1–2. Custer, E. B., *Tenting on the Plains*, 18.
3–4. Ibid., 21.
5–6. Barnett, *Touched by Fire: The Life, Death, and Mythic Afterlife of George Armstrong Custer*, 66.
7. Ibid., 67.
8. Utley, *Cavalier in Buckskin*, 38.
9. Merington, *The Custer Story*, 180.
10. Utley, *Cavalier in Buckskin*, 139.

11. Wert, *Custer*, 238.

12. Utley, *Cavalier in Buckskin*, 45.

13. Custer, E. B., *Tenting on the Plains*, 216.

14. Custer, G.A., *My Life on the Plains*, 25.

15. Prucha, *The Great Father: The United States Government and the American Indians*, 65.

16. Ibid., 71.

17. Senate Executive Document #26, 39th Congress, Serial #1277.

18. Senate Executive Document #33, 39th Congress, Serial #2504.

19. Senate Executive Document #26, 39th Congress, Serial #1277.

CHAPTER 5

1. Merington, *The Custer Story*, 199.

2. Wert, *Custer*, 251.

3. Monaghan, *Custer*, 285.

4. Wert, *Custer*, 253.

5–6. Kennedy, *On the Plains with Custer and Hancock: The Journal of Isaac Coates, Army Surgeon*, 26.

7. Custer, G. A., *My Life on the Plains*, 44–45.

8. Ibid., 38.

9. Ibid., 39.

10. Ibid., 40.

11. Ibid., 43.

12. Ibid., 44.

13. Ibid., 46.

14. Merington, *The Custer Story*, 199.

15. Custer, G. A., *My Life on the Plains*, 82.

CHAPTER 6

1. Custer, G. A., *My Life on the Plains*, 99.

2. Ibid., 100–102.

3. Ibid., 199.

4. Ibid., 198.

5. Utley, *Life in Custer's Cavalry: Diaries and Letters of Albert and Jennie Barnitz, 1867–1868*, 50.

6. Custer, G. A., *My Life on the Plains*, 128.

7. Ibid., 135.

8. Ibid., 142.

9. Utley, *Life in Custer's Cavalry*, 64.

10–11. Ibid., 56.

12. Hutton, *The Custer Reader*, 143.

Chapter 7

1. Hutton, *The Custer Reader*, 145.

2. Merington, *The Custer Story*, 212.

3. Utley, *Cavalier in Buckskin*, 57.

4–6. Collins, *The Cheyenne Wars Atlas*, 42.

7–8. Brady, *The Sioux Indian Wars*, 113.

9. Ibid., 114.

10. Custer, G. A., *My Life on the Plains*, 314.

11. Ibid., 315.

12. Ibid., 318.

13. Ibid., 320.

14. Utley, *Life in Custer's Cavalry*, 218.

15. Custer, G. A., *My Life on the Plains*, 331.

16. Hoig, *The Battle of the Washita*, 130–31.

17. Utley, *Life in Custer's Cavalry*, 226.

18. Custer, G. A., *My Life on the Plains*, 383.

19. Godfrey, "Some Reminiscences, Including the Washita Battle, November 27, 1868," *Cavalry Journal*.

20. Utley, *Cavalier in Buckskin*, 68.

21. Greene, *Washita: The US Army and the Southern Cheyenne, 1867–1869*, 102.

22. Hoig, *The Battle of the Washita*, 93.

23–24. Godfrey, "Some Reminiscences."

25. Hutton, *Phil Sheridan and His Army*, 79–80.

26–27. Graham, *The Custer Myth: A Source Book of Custeriana*, 208.

28. Wert, *Custer*, 287.

29–30. Custer, G. A., *My Life on the Plains*, 415.

CHAPTER 8

1–2. Crackel, "Custer's Kentucky," *Filson Club History Quarterly*.

3. Collins, *Atlas of the Sioux Wars*, 7.

4. Utley, *Cavalier in Buckskin*, 112.

5–6. Stanley, *Report on the Yellowstone Expedition of 1873*.

7. Custer, Elizabeth, *Boots and Saddles*, 69.

8. Hunt and Hunt, *I Fought with Custer: The Story of Sergeant Windolph, Last Survivor of the Battle of the Little Big Horn*, 6.

9. Monaghan, *Custer*, 343.

10. Stanley, *Yellowstone Expedition*.

11. Hutton, *The Custer Reader*, 209.

12. Ibid., 213.

13–16. Stanley, *Yellowstone Expedition*.

17. National Archives: Sioux Treaty of 1868 (online resource)

18. Merington, *The Custer Story*, 272.

19. Cozzens, *Eyewitnesses to the Indian Wars, 1865–1890*, 166.

20. Monaghan, *Custer*, 355.

21. Hatch, *The Custer Companion: A Comprehensive Guide to the Life of George Armstrong Custer and the Plains Indians Wars*, 148.

22. Merington, *The Custer Story*, 288.

CHAPTER 9

1–2. *Courier-Journal*, July 4, 1876.

3–6. Collins, "The Great Sioux War of 1876–77," *Atlas of the Sioux Wars*, No. 3.

7. Custer, E. B., *Boots and Saddles*, 207.

8. Ibid., 218.

9. Ibid., 222.

10. F. F. Girard testimony, Official Record of the Reno Court of Inquiry (hereafter referred to as "Reno Court").

11. Godfrey, "Custer's Last Battle," *The Century*, January 1892.

12. Graham, *The Custer Myth*, 300.

13–14. Godfrey, "Custer's Last Battle."

15. Girard testimony, Reno Court.

16–17. Stewart, *Custer's Luck*, 259, 263.

18. Godfrey, "Custer's Last Battle."

19. Hunt and Hunt, *I Fought With Custer*, 74.

Chapter 10

1. Graham, " 'Come on! Be quick! Bring packs!' The Story of Custer's Last Message," *Cavalry Journal*.

2. Stewart, *Custer's Luck*, 275.

3. Coughlan, "A Tactical Study of the Bighorn Campaign," *Cavalry Journal*.

4. Graham, *The Custer Myth*, 179.

5. Graham, "'Come on! Be quick! Bring packs!'"

6. Benteen testimony, Reno Court.

7–8. Hunt and Hunt, *I Fought with Custer*, 76.

9–11. Benteen testimony, Reno Court.

12. Hunt and Hunt, *I Fought with Custer*, 78.

13. Girard testimony, Reno Court.

14–15. Hunt and Hunt, *I Fought with Custer*, 82.

16–17. Taylor, *With Custer on the Little Bighorn*, 36.

18. Graham, *The Custer Myth*, 241.

19. Varnum testimony, Reno Court.

20–21. Reno Court.

22. *St. Paul Pioneer Press*, July 18, 1886.

23. Moylan testimony, Reno Court.

24. Herendeen testimony, Reno Court.

25. Wallace testimony, Reno Court.

26. Varnum testimony, Reno Court.

27. Dr. Porter testimony, Reno Court.

28. Girard testimony, Reno Court.

29. Girard testimony, Reno Court.

30. Graham, *The Custer Myth*, 242.

31. Varnum testimony, Reno Court.

32. Marquis, *Wooden Leg: A Warrior Who Fought Custer*, 221.

33. Reno testimony, Reno Court.

34. Dr. Porter testimony, Reno Court.

35. Herendeen testimony, Reno Court.

CHAPTER 11

1. Graham, *The Custer Myth*, 249.

2–3. Benteen testimony, Reno Court.

4. Fox, *Archaeology, History, and Custer's Last Battle: The Little Big Horn Reexamined*, 139, 243.

5. Connell, *Son of the Morning Star*, 390.

6. Ibid., 413.

7. Merington, *The Custer Story*, 98, 143.

8. Varnum testimony, Reno Court.

9. Godfrey testimony, Reno Court.

10. Graham, *The Custer Myth*, 200.

11. Benteen testimony, Reno Court.

12. Varnum testimony, Reno Court.

13. Hunt and Hunt, *I Fought With Custer*, 101.

14. Stewart, *Custer's Luck*, 409.

15. Wallace testimony, Reno Court.

16. Edgerly testimony, Reno Court.

17. Herendeen testimony, Reno Court.

18–19. Wallace testimony, Reno Court.

20. Godfrey, "Custer's Last Battle."

21. Edgerly testimony, Reno Court.

22. Wallace testimony, Reno Court.

23. Graham, *The Custer Myth*, 192.

24–26. *Courier-Journal*, July 7, 1876.

27–28. *Louisville Daily Commercial*, July 8, 1876.

BIBLIOGRAPHY

BOOKS AND MAGAZINES

Barnett, Louise. *Touched by Fire: The Life, Death, and Mythic Afterlife of George Armstrong Custer.* New York: Henry Holt & Co., 1996.

Brady, Cyrus Townsend. *Indian Fights and Fighters.* Lincoln, NE: Bison Books, 1971.

———. *The Sioux Indian Wars.* New York: Indian Head Books, 1992.

Brininstool, E. A. *Troopers with Custer.* New York: Bonanza Books, 1952.

Carroll, John M. *Custer in the Civil War: His Unfinished Memoirs.* San Rafael, CA: Presidio, 1977.

Collins, Charles D. *Atlas of the Sioux Wars.* Fort Leavenworth, KS: Combat Studies Institute Press, 2006.

———. *The Cheyenne Wars Atlas.* Fort Leavenworth, KS: Combat Studies Institute Press, 2006.

Connell, Evan S. *Son of the Morning Star.* San Francisco, CA: North Point Press, 1984.

Coughlan, Colonel T. M. "A Tactical Study of the Bighorn Campaign," *Cavalry Journal,* vol. 43, no. 181, January–February, 1934.

Cozzens, Peter. *Eyewitnesses to the Indian Wars, 1865–1890.* Mechanicsburg, PA: Stackpole Books, 2001.

Crackel, Theodore J. "Custer's Kentucky," *Filson Club History Quarterly,* vol. 49, April 1974.

Custer, Elizabeth B. *Boots and Saddles.* New York: Harper and Brothers, 1885.

———. *Tenting on the Plains.* New York: Harper and Brothers, 1887.

Custer, George Armstrong. *My Life on the Plains.* Norman: University of Oklahoma Press, 1874, 1962.

Fox, Richard A. *Archaeology, History, and Custer's Last Battle: The Little Big Horn Reexamined.* Norman: University of Oklahoma Press, 1993.

Frost, Lawrence A. *The Custer Album: A Pictorial Biography of George Armstrong Custer.* Norman: University of Oklahoma Press, 1990.

Godfrey, Edward S. "Custer's Last Battle," *The Century,* January 1892.

———. "Some Reminiscences, Including the Washita Battle, November 27, 1868," *Cavalry Journal,* vol. 37, no. 153, October 1928.

Graham, Colonel W. A. "'Come on! Be quick! Bring packs!' The Story of Custer's Last Message," *Cavalry Journal,* vol. 32, July 1923.

———. *The Custer Myth: A Source Book of Custeriana.* New York: Bonanza Books, 1953.

Greene, Jerome A. *Washita: The US Army and the Southern Cheyenne, 1867–1869.* Norman: University of Oklahoma Press, 2004.

Hatch, Thom. *The Custer Companion: A Comprehensive Guide to the Life of George Armstrong Custer and the Plains Indian Wars.* Mechanicsburg, PA: Stackpole Books, 2002.

Hofling, Charles K. *Custer and the Little Big Horn: A Psychobiographical Inquiry.* Detroit: Wayne State University Press, 1981.

Hoig, Stan. *The Battle of the Washita.* Garden City, NY: Doubleday, 1976.

———. *The Sand Creek Massacre.* Norman: University of Oklahoma Press, 1961.

Hunt, Frazier, and Robert Hunt. *I Fought with Custer: The Story of Sergeant Windolph, Last Survivor of the Battle of the Little Big Horn.* New York: Charles Scribner's Sons, 1947.

Hutton, Paul Andrew, ed. *The Custer Reader.* Lincoln: University of Nebraska Press, 1992.

———. *Phil Sheridan and His Army.* Norman: University of Oklahoma Press, 1999.

Keim, De Benneville Randolph. *Sheridan's Troopers on the Borders.* Philadelphia: David McKay, 1891.

Kennedy, W. J. D., ed. *On the Plains with Custer and Hancock: The Journal of Isaac Coates, Army Surgeon*. Boulder, CO: Johnson Books, 1997.

Kinsley, D. A. *Custer: Favor the Bold, A Soldier's Story*. New York: Promontory Press, 1967.

———. *Favor the Bold: Custer, the Indian Fighter*. New York: Promontory Press, 1968.

Longstreet, James. *From Manassas to Appomattox*. Philadelphia: J. B. Lippincott, 1908.

Marquis, Thomas B. *Wooden Leg: A Warrior Who Fought Custer*. Lincoln: University of Nebraska Press, 1962.

McPherson, James M. *Battle Cry of Freedom*. New York: Oxford University Press, 1988.

Merington, Marguerite, ed. *The Custer Story: The Life and Intimate Letters of General George A. Custer and His Wife Elizabeth*. New York: Devin-Adair, 1950.

Miller, David Humphreys. *Custer's Fall*. New York: Duell, Sloan and Pearce, 1957.

Monaghan, Jay. *Custer: The Life of General George Armstrong Custer*. Lincoln: University of Nebraska Press, 1959.

Nevin, David. *The Old West: The Soldiers*. New York: Time-Life Books, 1973.

Prucha, Francis Paul. *The Great Father: The United States Government and the American Indians*. Lincoln: University of Nebraska Press, 1984.

Sears, Stephen W. *George B. McClellan: The Young Napoleon*. New York: Ticknor & Fields, 1988.

Stanley, David Sloane. *Report on the Yellowstone Expedition of 1873*. Washington, DC: Library of Congress, 1874.

Stewart, Edgar I. *Custer's Luck*. Norman: University of Oklahoma Press, 1955.

Taylor, William O. *With Custer on the Little Bighorn*. New York: Viking, 1996.

Urwin, Gregory J. W. *Custer Victorious: The Civil War Battles of General George Armstrong Custer*. East Brunswick, NJ: Associated University Presses, 1983.

Utley, Robert M. *Cavalier in Buckskin*. Norman: University of Oklahoma Press, 1988.

———., ed. *Life in Custer's Cavalry: Diaries and Letters of Albert and Jennie Barnitz, 1867–1868*. New Haven: Yale University Press, 1977.

Van de Water, Frederic F. *Glory-Hunter: A Life of General Custer*. Lincoln: University of Nebraska Press, 1988.

Wert, Jeffry D. *Custer: The Controversial Life of George Armstrong Custer*. New York: Simon & Schuster, 1996.

NEWSPAPERS

Bismarck Tribune Extra

Chicago Times

Courier-Journal (Louisville)

Louisville Daily Commercial

New York Herald

New York Times

St. Paul Pioneer Press

OTHER DOCUMENTS

National Archives.

National Park Service.

The Official Record of the Reno Court of Inquiry.

Senate Executive Document #26, 39th Congress, Serial #1277.

Senate Executive Document #33, 39th Congress, Serial #2504.

INDEX

alcohol consumption in military, 58,
    79, 119–20
Alexandria, Louisiana, troops in,
    47–49
Anaconda, 19–20
Appomattox Campaign, 41
Arapaho Tribe, 64, 66. *See also* Plains
    Indians
Arikaree River encampment, 95
artillery. *See* firearms

Bacon, Daniel, 29–32
Bacon, Elizabeth. *See* Custer, Libbie
    (Bacon)
Baliran, Augustus, 126
Ball, Private, 126
balloon observations, 21–22
Barnitz, Albert, 78, 85, 102, 105–6
Barnitz, Jennie, 86
Beauregard, Pierre G. T., 15, 16–17
Beecher, Frederick H., 94, 96
Beecher's Island, 97
Belknap, William W., 133–34
Benteen, Frederick
    bravery in battle, 176–77, 187–88
    buffalo hunting by, 77
    criticism of Marcus Reno, 185–87
    defiance of Custer, 167
    dislike of Custer, 78, 87, 187
    humiliation of Custer, 110–12
    killing of Blue Horse by, 104–5
    letter to widow of Custer, 145
    message to Tom Custer, 167
    note from W. W. Cooke, 166

Bismarck Tribune Extra, 179–83
Black Hills
    exploration of, 129
    gold discovery, 116–17,
        129–32, 136
    sacredness of, 128
    See also Dakota Territory
Black Horse Cavalry, 18
Black Kettle, Chief
    Battle of Washita River and, 97–98,
        99, 104, 106, 108, 109–10,
        112, 187
    death of nephew, 104–5
    Sand Creek Massacre and,
        58–59, 75
Blinn, Clara, 110
Blinn, Willi, 110
Bloody Knife, x, 146, 152, 161, 162
Blue Horse, 104–5
Bowen (topographical engineer), 23
Boyer, Mitch, 146
Bradley, James H., 138
buffalo hunting, 73–74, 77
bugle calls/buglers, 61, 81, 82,
    100, 111, 149, 152, 161–62,
    174, 186
Bull Run Creek, 17
Bull Run, First Battle of (First
    Manassas), 16–19

Calhoun, James, 123, 170, 178
Calhoun, Margaret, 143
California Joe (scout), 99
Carrington, Henry B., 60–62

ABOUT THE AUTHOR

Kevin Sullivan is the author of *The Bundy Murders: A Comprehensive History*. He is also a former contributing writer for *Snitch*, a paper that was at one time published in five states, devoted to issues of crime and the law.